I0093849

George Saintsbury

Political Verse

George Saintsbury

Political Verse

ISBN/EAN: 9783337072971

Printed in Europe, USA, Canada, Australia, Japan

Cover: Foto ©Suzi / pixelio.de

More available books at **www.hansebooks.com**

Demy 16mo, 3s. 6d. each.
Bound in paper boards, with parchment back.

THE POCKET LIBRARY

OF

ENGLISH LITERATURE

EDITED BY GEORGE SAINTSBURY

A COLLECTION, in separate volumes, partly of extracts from long books, partly of short pieces, by the same writer, on the same subject, or of the same class.

LONDON : PERCIVAL & CO.

EDITED BY

GEORGE SAINTSBURY

LONDON
PERCIVAL AND CO.
1891

CONTENTS

Contents

MARK AKENSIDE

CHARLES CHURCHILL

WILLIAM COWPER

'THE ROLLIAD'

PETER PINDAR

'THE ANTI-JACOBIN'

SIR WALTER SCOTT

GEORGE CANNING

Contents

LORD BYRON

THOMAS MOORE

Contents

Contents xiii

INTRODUCTION

It is at first sight curious, at second perhaps intelligible enough, that (unless I am entirely deceived) no special collection of the political verse of different periods in England has ever been attempted. Some such verse—*The Rolliad*, Peter Pindar's best things, those of Moore and Praed—have been very popular in their own time. Once at least, in the case of *The Poetry of the Anti-Jacobin*, they have reached more than temporary popularity. But no one has, I think, yet attempted an anthology of them. One reason for this may be that they require, or are thought to require, a rather unusual amount of scholiastic annotation to render them intelligible to generations not their own; another, that in some cases at any rate the ashes of the fires that once burnt are either still too hot for safe treading, or so utterly cold and dead that to tramp through them is toilsome and disgusting. Often too, when indignation has made verses of this kind, it has made them a little carelessly. The most ferocious and not the least vigorous political poem that I know, the *Prosa cleri Parisiensis*, which was written by some Huguenot (I hope it was Agrippa d'Aubigné) on the murder of Henri III. by Jacques Clément, suffers from this roughness particularly. But we have in England, in old times and in new, not a little most excellent verse, which is free from this defect, and from another, that of coarseness, which disfigures not only the piece I have mentioned but a great deal of French political verse and some English, from Rochester's certainly to Wolcot's, and perhaps to Canning's. Of this it should be possible to make a not uncomely or uninteresting fascicle, the chief difficulty in the binding whereof must be the giving of sufficient information for understanding the pieces without burdening the volume with notes unsuited in length and tenor both to its size and to its purpose. I hope I may not be too unsuccessful in surmounting this difficulty, or too niggardly (none, I think, will think me too profuse) in explanation.

It is seldom that political verse is very early : in English it is, at least such as has attained to any

polish and merit, decidedly late. Nor are the reasons
of this hard to understand. In the first place, such
verse is, in the straightforward manners of personally-
governed and not very elaborately civilised nations, a
decidedly dangerous amusement. The sovereign and
his representatives do not understand raillery addressed to themselves, and have little use for it as
applied to others, who are better disciplined with axe
and fetter, gallows and scourge. Politics, moreover,
at such times are too much matters of earnest; not
to mention that until printing is invented and toler-
ably free there is no means of securing any wider
public than that which can crowd round Pasquin's
statue. Accordingly but little will be found here
of earlier date than the seventeenth century, and
that little is very rude in both senses of the word.
Although it is not wholly political in application,
and so does not find place here, Sir Walter
Raleigh's 'Lie,'—for he pretty certainly wrote it,
though quite certainly not on the night before his
execution,—is one of the first polished pieces of the
kind that we have. There was no Agrippa d'Aubigné
among our reformers; and their successors, the Puri-
tans, were not verse-smiths, though the prose of
Martin Marprelate is in its bludgeonly way as

effective a weapon as can well be conceived. This aversion to verse lasted during the great political dissension of the middle of the century, and made the contest too one-sided to be very equal. Bishop Corbet is perhaps the best anti-Puritan rhymester, and taking ecclesiastical matters as a branch of politics, I shall be able to give some good specimens from him and from one or two others. But as I wish to exhibit not so much the elaborate satire, the three-decker of political verse (though we must have a broadside or two from her also now and then) as lighter craft, I shall draw but sparingly on this period.

The next, that of the last two Stuarts, is somewhat richer, and naturally so, for all the conditions were becoming more favourable to the kind. The fight, though still sharp, and still opening up prospects of the scaffold in one direction and the pillory in another, was by this time a little less internecine. Party, the great tonic and stimulant of political verse, was forming itself, and, moreover, the general style and tenor of literature and the literary spirit were becoming more and more favourable. As the spring of poetry proper ebbed in the nation, so did that of what has been called applied poetry flow all the more briskly. The interesting collection called the *State*

Poems, supplemented by the more regular works of divers distinguished writers, supplies abundant instances of all kinds of exercises in the style, from verse so vigorous and polished, that it deserves the name of poetry down to the lowest doggerel. In no kind did the genius of Dryden show itself better, and though I have never been able to convince myself that the 'Young Statesmen' is his, it has never been credibly assigned to any one else, and is one of the first, and not one of the worst, political lyrics extant in English. Rochester's wilful and disgusting coarseness mars some excellent exercises of his in the line—a drawback which extends to a much more respectable person, Marvell, and to not a few others. There is still, moreover, too much venom in the ink, and perhaps only Dryden achieves what is the very first requisite in political verse—the assumption rather of an easy and amused disdain than of a stern and prophetic indignation at the adversary. It may be laid down that the first object of political verse should be to make the foe ridiculous, and that the making of him detestable should be a secondary and cunningly concealed consequence. The early satirists, for the most part, too much forget this.

The next age of political verse, which may be said

to run from the Revolution to about 1780, shows something of the same features as that which we have just noticed, but with differences. The Drydenian satire was very commonly imitated, and latterly had much of the weakness, if something also of the accomplishment, of a stock literary form. Akenside, Churchill, and others exhibited both these characteristics of it. It might seem that no two men ever existed so proper for the style as Swift and Pope, but Pope was utterly unprovided with a political head ; his political interests were purely personal, and though he is constantly, so to speak, on the outskirts of political verse, he never quite attains to it. Swift understood politics thoroughly, and was a master, if not of poetry, of verse both light and serious ; but he too has never reached the acme, such things as 'The Legion Club' being again too purely personal. Prior, more superficial and less impassioned, did somewhat better, but not much, and his best things are in far other styles. In substance *The True-born Englishman* perhaps excels anything by these men ; but Defoe lacked poetic grace of form too utterly to enter into competition with them. Over all the political verse-writers of this period there is a certain constraint, to be accounted for, perhaps, by the half-foreign character of national politics under the Dutchman and the Hanoverians—by the tortuous and unworthy intrigues of the reign of Anne. Nevertheless there is much noteworthy work here to be got hold of, and Akenside especially is far too generally forgotten. Yet perhaps the happiest thing of the time is the famous epitaph on Prince Frederick, which has all the best notes—ease, contempt, brevity, bitterness, point. It looks facile enough—most very good things do— but I do not think that it is quite so easy as it looks. At any rate I wish I had written it, and that is perhaps as fair a criterion of goodness as is attainable in such a matter. On the whole, however, considering the character and genius of the age, the opportunities of political satire which were afforded by the peculiarities of the reigning family and of the party warfare of the time, and the remarkable amount of literary talent which was disposable, I think the first three-quarters of the eighteenth century were rather less fertile in good political verse than might have been expected.

No such complaint can possibly be made of the time which succeeded. It may be that the increasing whole-heartedness of national politics after George the Third took away the reproach of the 'wee, wee

German lairdies' from us, had something to do with
it.   It may be, to take a less heroic view, that the
sense that there was no serious danger now to be
feared by the political satirist had as much, or more.
Certainly the years, though in point of actual time
not far distant, when St. John raged among the unlucky Whig pressmen were far off.   Even in the more
tolerant days of the *ancien régime* (and they were,
on the whole, much more tolerant than ignorance
thinks them) Wolcot could hardly have lived a whole
year of his life out of the Bastille in France ; and the
wits of *The Rolliad*, unless they had resorted to
clandestine presses and imprints of 'Monomotapa'
and the like, would have had an unhappy time if
they had treated any French minister as Lawrence
and Fitzpatrick and the rest treated Pitt.   Very
hardly, again, would the ministerial side have enlisted
in a less free country, and with the national feeling less
thoroughly engaged on the side of the Government,
such support as that of Canning and Ellis and Frere
and North.   In the work of the earlier or Whig group
ingenious coterie-depreciation, personal tittle-tattle,
and the like, are applied to political verse in a way
which has never been surpassed.   In the work of the
later or Tory group the weapons of a generous and

patriotic satire were put into the hands of authority
as they never had been before; and perhaps, all
things considered, as they never have been since.
For the society of that day offered advantages to the
political satirist which earlier he had not attained,
and which since he has, to some extent, lost.   The
reading public was not inconsiderable in numbers,
but it was not unmanageably large.   It was spread
with some evenness all over England.   It was not
subdivided by any minor fads and parties, but was,
on the whole, either frankly Whig or frankly Tory.
It had great political power, being, as a rule, con-
terminous with the not widely-separated limits of the
franchise.   It had all been educated very much in
the same way, understood the same allusions, caught
the same innuendoes.   (It has sometimes been con-
tended, and I own that it is my opinion, that the so-
called spread of education has diluted the strength
and liveliness as much as it has enlarged the volume
of the national intelligence.)   Again, there was little
foreign news; nor was the attention distracted by
multifarious domestic details in such newspapers as
there were.   A thing might take weeks or months to
penetrate, where it now arrives in a day; but it was
certain of an attentive audience wherever it did

penetrate, instead of being forgotten almost before
it is read.   The author even of an epigram on a
subject of public interest knew that sooner or later
almost everybody who read and thought in Great
Britain would hear of it, enjoy it, or be annoyed by
it.   Add to this the unparalleled interest first of the
great party struggle which lifted the Tory party after
sixty years of depression to the control of English
affairs, and then of the greater war which made
Britain first the champion and then the arbiter of
Europe, and it can hardly be wondered that the
political verse of this period is of such merit.   It was
forced by events, and, like most sturdy plants, it
bore the forcing well.   No space here at my command could suffice to do it justice in detail, but the
extracts from it will speak, and perhaps its still green
fame, as a whole, will speak still better.   Undoubtedly
1780-1800 was the Augustan age of English political
verse.   Nor will it surprise any one who has studied
the laws of poetical production to remark that it
was at the same time almost a dead season, with rare
exceptions of promise and performance, in verse not
political.

It cannot, however, be said that in the fresh
blossoming time of poetry proper which followed,

political verse showed any considerable signs of decadence. Canning continued to write it more or less till his death. On the other side, Moore (perhaps the best political verse-writer whom that side has produced), began about the end of the first decade of the present century to write most agreeable things of the kind, and continued to do so for thirty years and more. As Canning's day was done a new and charming writer, first for a brief space on the Whig, then for much longer on the Tory side, introduced a fresh flavour into the style. Winthrop Mackworth Praed wrote in a fashion more scholarly than Moore's and less ferocious than Canning's, and shows something like supremacy in his own vein. During the last half-century the bulk of political, as of other verse which has been written, has been very great, and perhaps the abundance of it has a little injured the quality. But in the third quarter Thackeray ought to have been a political verse-writer of the very first order, and if he was not the reason is probably to be found in the fact that he had neither any very definite conception of politics as a science, nor any clear and decided attachment to a political party. Nominally a Liberal, and strictly maintaining certain Liberal doctrines, he was in tastes, sentiment, historical predilections, and intellectual temper a strong though a whimsical Tory. To which it may be added, that his too brief life did not make him the contemporary of any great political struggle except that of the Corn Laws, which was barren soil enough for grass of Parnassus to grow on. He was too young at the date of the first Reform Bill to feel much interest in politics; he died before the death of Lord Palmerston opened a new era of conflict. In that era at least one admirable writer, the only one of living men on whom it has seemed necessary to me to draw—Mr. H. D. Traill—has appeared, and quite recently his example has stirred up others.

A few general 'collections,' in the old logical sense of the term, from this survey and our extracts may be allowed to speak for themselves. We have said that political verse is a rather late product; we may see further that though, as has also been said, it is necessary that it should be written not too seriously in appearance, some great stir of the general mind is almost invariably required in order to produce it. The life-and-death struggles of the Popish Plot; the astonishment and disgust of the reigning Whig aristocracy at the uprising of a Tory interloper like Pitt, and the rallying round him of a new party; the frenzy of the French Revolution; the assault upon the limited franchise by the middle class first, and then by the nation at large; the attempts which have been made of latest years to change the entire tradition of English policy and government at home and abroad—these are the hotbeds in which such flowers grow. If sometimes they seem to have a more limited origin (such as in the unique and admirable work of the late Dean Mansel on University Reform) it must be remembered that university politics have always been of a specially warm kind, and that here general politics come in as well. Yet another point is that political verse is, for the most part, written best if not written only by men of very considerable cultivation. Ebenezer Elliotts and persons of that kind are rare exceptions, and generally fail in the command of temper, the apparent, if not real, detachment which has been noted above as almost, if not quite, indispensable. Perhaps this last point may have something to do with another which I may be thought likely to exaggerate, owing to some personal partisanship. I refer to the curious fact that, even more than political satire in general, political verse satire is apt to be written on the side of order, as it is called, and authority rather

than on that of what is called liberty and progress.
The reasons for this each man must supply for
himself. It is too dangerous a subject for me
to enter upon.

Phrontisterion, Sc. iii., is inserted by the kind
permission of Mr. John Murray: *King Canute* by
that of Messrs. Smith, Elder, and Co.

LIBRARY
OF THE
UNIVERSITY
OF
CALIFORNIA

JOHN SKELTON

(Except in acrimony, the following piece from Why Come ye not to Courte? *is an ill foot to put foremost in a selection of political verse. It is, however, almost necessary as a specimen of the infancy of the art in England, and not uninteresting as an example of the kind of verse with which such an indignation as that commonly felt against Wolsey inspired such a wit as Skelton's.)*

CARDINAL WOLSEY

ONCE yet agayn
Of you I wold fraine
Why come ye not to courte?
   To which court?
To the Kinges court
Or to Hampton court?
   Nay to the Kinges court
The Kynges court

Should haue the excellence
But Hampton court
Hath the preeminence
And Yorkes place
With my lordes grace
To whose magnificence
Is all the confluence
Sutes and applications
Embassades of all nacions
Straw for law canon
Or for the law common
Or for law ciuill
It shall be as he wyll
Stop at law tancrete
An abstract or a concrete
Be it soure be it sweete
His wisdome is so discrete
That in a fume or an hete
Warden of the Flete
Set him fast by the fete
And of his royal poure
Whan him lyst to loure
Then haue him to the Toure
Saunz aulter remedy
Haue him forth by and by
To the Marshalsy
Or to the Kinges benche
He diggeth so in the trench

Of the court royall
That he ruleth them all
So he dothe undermynde
And such sleights doth fynde
That the Kinges mynde
By him is subuerted
And so streatly coarted
In credensing his tales
That al is but nutshales
That any other sayth
He hath in him such faith
  Now, yet al this might be
Suffred and taken in gree
If that, that he wrought
To any good end wer brought
But all he bryngeth to nought
But God that me deare bought
  He beareth the king on hand
That he must pyl his land
To make his cofers rych
But he layeth al in the dyche
And useth such abusion
That in the conclusion
All commeth to confusion
Perceiue the cause whye
To tell the trouth plainlye
He is so ambicious
So shameless, and so vicious

And so supersticious
And so much obliuious
From whens that he came
That he falleth in Acisiam
Which truely to expresse
Is a forgetfulnes
Or wylful blyndnes
Wherwith the Sodomites
Lost their inward sightes
    The Gommorians also
Were brought to deadly wo
As scripture recordes
A cecitate cordis
In the Latin sygne we
Libera nos Domine
    But this mad Amalecke
Like to Amamelek
He regardeth lordes
No more than pot shordes
He is in suche elacion
Of his exaltacion
And the supportacion
Of our soueraine lorde
That God to recorde
He ruleth al at will
Without reason or skyll
Howbeit they be prymordyall
Of hys wretched originall

Cardinal Wolsey

And his base progeny
And his gresy genealogy
He came of the sanke roiall
That was cast out of a bouchers stall.
    But howe euer he was borne
Men would haue the lesse scorne
If he could consider
His byrth and rowme together
And call to his mynde
How noble and how kynde
To hym he hath founde
Our souerayne lord, chief grounde
Of all thys prelacy
And set hym nobly
In great aucthorite
Out from a low degre
Which he can not see
For he was parde
No doctour of divinite
Nor doctor of the law
Nor of none other saw
But a pore maister of arte
God wot had little part
Of the quatriuials
Nor yet of triuials
Nor of philosophye
Nor of philology
Nor of good pollicy

John Skelton

Nor of astronomy
Nor acquainted worth a fly
With honourable Italy
Nor with royal Ptholomy
Nor with Albumasar
To treate of any star
Fyxt or els mobil
His Latin tongue doth hobbyl
He doth but clout and cobbel
In Tullis facultie
Called humanitie
Yet proudly he dare pretend
How no man can him amend
But haue ye not heard this
How a one-eyed man is
Wel sighted, wen
He is amonge blynd men.

EDMUND SPENSER

(Prosopopoia : or Mother Hubberd's Tale, *is gener-*
ally and rightly quoted as a very early example of true
satire in English verse.   To that exercise Spenser (as not
only this poem but many passages in The Shepheard's
Calender, *in the* Faërie Queene *herself, and elsewhere*
show) had considerable inclination.   If any one questions
the exact appropriateness of the piece here, let him remem-
ber that there were no such burning questions of State in
the sixteenth century as questions touching the Church.)

THE POLITIC CLERK

THE Priest gan wexe halfe proud to be so praide,
And thereby willing to affoord them aide ;
' It seemes (said he) right well that ye be Clerks,
Both by your wittie words, and by your werks.
Is not that name enough to make a living
To him that hath a whit of Natures giving ?
How manie honest men see ye arize

Daylie thereby, and grow to goodly prize ;
To Deanes, to Archdeacons, to Commissaries,
To Lords, to Principalls, to Prebendaries ?
All jolly Prelates, worthie rule to beare,
Who ever them envie : yet spite bites neare.
Why should ye doubt, then, but that ye likewise
Might unto some of those in time arise ?
In the meane-time to live in good estate,
Loving that love, and hating those that hate ;
Being some honest Curate, or some Vicker
Content with little in condition sicker.'
'Ah ! but (said th' Ape) the charge is wondrous great,
To feed mens soules, and hath an heavie threat.'
'To feede mens soules (quoth he) is not in man ;
For they must feed themselves, doo what we can.
We are but charg'd to lay the meate before :
Eate they that list, we need to doo no more.
But God it is that feedes them with his grace,
The bread of life powr'd downe from heavenly place.
Therefore said he, that with the budding rod
Did rule the Jewes, *All shalbe taught of God.*
That same hath Jesus Christ now to him raught,
By whom the flock is rightly fed, and taught :
He is the Shepheard, and the Priest is hee ;
We but his shepheard swaines ordain'd to bee.
Therefore herewith doo not your selfe dismay ;
Ne is the paines so great, but beare ye may,
For not so great, as it was wont of yore,

The Politic Clerk

It's now a dayes, ne halfe so streight and sore.
They whilome used duly everie day
Their service and their holie things to say,
At morne and even, besides their Anthemes sweete,
Their penie Masses, and their Complynes meete,
Their Diriges, their Trentals, and their shrifts,
Their memories, their singings, and their gifts.
Now all those needlesse works are laid away;
Now once a weeke, upon the Sabbath day,
It is enough to doo our small devotion,
And then to follow any merrie motion.
Ne are we tyde to fast, but when we list;
Ne to weare garments base of wollen twist,
But with the finest silkes us to aray,
That before God we may appeare more gay,
Resembling Aarons glorie in his place:
For farre unfit it is, that person bace
Should with vile cloaths approach Gods majestie,
Whom no uncleannes may approachen nie;
Or that all men, which anie master serve,
Good garments for their service should deserve;
But he that serves the Lord of hoasts most high,
And that in highest place, t' approach him nigh,
And all the peoples prayers to present
Before his throne, as on ambassage sent
Both too and fro, should not deserve to weare
A garment better than of wooll or heare.
Beside, we may have lying by our sides

Our lovely Lasses, or bright shining Brides :
We be not tyde to wilfull chastitie,
But have the Gospell of free libertie.'
　　By that he ended had his ghostly sermon,
The Foxe was well induc'd to be a Parson,
And of the Priest eftsoones gan to enquire,
How to a Benefice he might aspire ?
' Marie, there (said the Priest) is arte indeed :
Much good deep learning one thereout may reed ;
For that the ground-worke is, and end of all,
How to obtaine a Beneficiall.
First, therefore, when ye have in handsome wise
Your selfe attyred, as you can devise,
Then to some Noble-man your selfe applye,
Or other great one in the worldës eye,
That hath a zealous disposition
To God, and so to his religion.
There must thou fashion eke a godly zeale,
Such as no carpers may contrayre reveale ;
For each thing fained ought more warie bee.
There thou must walke in sober gravitee,
And seeme as Saintlike as Saint Radegund :
Fast much, pray oft, looke lowly on the ground,
And unto everie one doo curtesie meeke :
These lookes (nought saying) doo a benefice seeke,
And be thou sure one not to lacke or long.
But if thee list unto the Court to throng,
And there to hunt after the hoped pray,

Then must thou thee dispose another way:
For there thou needs must learne to laugh, to lie,
To face, to forge, to scoffe, to companie,
To crouche, to please, to be a beetle-stock
Of thy great Masters will, to scorne, or mock.
So maist thou chaunce mock out a Benefice,
Unlesse thou canst one conjure by device,
Or cast a figure for a Bishoprick;
And if one could, it were but a schoole trick.
These be the wayes by which without reward
Livings in Court be gotten, though full hard;
For nothing there is done without a fee:
The Courtier needes must recompenced bee
With a Benevolence, or have in gage
The Primitias of your Parsonage:
Scarse can a Bishoprick forpas them by,
But that it must be gelt in privitie.
Doo not thou therefore seeke a living there,
But of more private persons seeke elswhere,
Whereas thou maist compound a better penie,
Ne let thy learning question'd be of anie.
For some good Gentleman, that hath the right
Unto his Church for to present a wight,
Will cope with thee in reasonable wise;
That if the living yerely doo arise
To fortie pound, that then his youngest sonne
Shall twentie have, and twentie thou hast wonne:
Thou hast it wonne, for it is of franke gift,

And he will care for all the rest to shift,
Both that the Bishop may admit of thee,
And that therein thou maist maintained bee.
This is the way for one that is unlern'd
Living to get, and not to be discern'd.
But they, that are great Clerkes, have nearer wayes,
For learning sake to living them to raise;
Yet manie eke of them (God wote) are driven
T' accept a Benefice in peeces riven.
How saist thou (friend) have I not well discourst
Upon this Common-place, (though plaine, not wourst?)
Better a short tale than a bad long shriving:
Needes anie more to learne to get a living?'

BISHOP CORBET

(This excellent satire was probably inspired in Corbet, one of the lightest and brightest wits of his time, almost equally by High Churchmanship, Toryism —for though the name was later the thing existed,— and the partisanship of an Oxford man.)

THE DISTRACTED PURITANE

Am I madd, O noble Festus,
When zeale and godly knowledge
    Have put me in hope
    To deal with the pope,
  As well as the best in the colledge?
Boldly I preach, hate a crosse, hate a surplice,
  Miters, copes, and rochets:
Come heare me pray nine times a day,
  And fill your heads with crochets.

In the house of pure Emanuel
I had my education ;
    Where my friends surmise
    I dazzled my eyes
With the light of revelation.
Boldly I preach, etc.

They bound me like a Bedlam,
They lash't my foure poore quarters ;
    Whilst this I endure,
    Faith makes me sure
To be one of Foxe's martyrs.
Boldly I preach, etc.

These injuryes I suffer
Through anti-Christs' perswasions :
    Take off this chaine,
    Neither Rome nor Spaine
Can resist my strong invasions.
Boldly I preach, etc.

Of the beast's ten hornes (God blesse us !)
I have knock't off three already :
    If they let me alone,
    I'll leave him none ;
But they say I'm too heady.
Boldly I preach, etc.

When I sack'd the seaven-hill'd citty
I mett the great redd dragon :
    I kept him aloofe
    With the armour of proofe,
Though here I have never a rag one.
Boldly I preach, etc.

With a fiery sword and targett
There fought I with this monster :
    But the sonnes of pride
    My zeale deride,
And all my deedes misconster.
Boldly I preach, etc.

I unhorst the whore of Babel
With a launce of inspirations :
    I made her stinke,
    And spill her drinck
In the cupp of abominations.
Boldly I preach, etc.

I have seen two in a vision,
With a flying booke betweene them :
    I have bin in despaire
    Five times a yeare
And cur'd by reading Greenham.
Boldly I preach, etc.

I observ'd in Perkin's Tables
The black lines of damnation :
Those crooked veines
Soe struck in my braines,
That I fear'd my reprobation.
Boldly I preach, etc.

In the holy tongue of Chanaan
I plac'd my chiefest pleasure :
Till I prickt my foote
With an Hebrew roote,
That I bledd beyond all measure.
Boldly I preach, etc.

I appear'd before the arch-bishop,
And all the high commission :
I gave him noe grace,
But told him to his face
That he favour'd superstition.
Boldly I preach, hate a crosse, hate a surplice
Miters, copes, and rochets :
Come heare me pray nine times a day,
And fill your heads with crochets.

ALEXANDER BROME

(Brome was a good cavalier, and an Anacreontic singer of some merit. His satire on the parliament's proceedings, though deficient in form, is fairly sharp.)

THE LEVELLER'S RANT

To the hall, to the hall,
For justice we call,
On the king and his pow'rful adherents and friends,
Who still have endeavour'd, but we work their ends.
'Tis we will pull down whate'er is above us,
And make them to fear us, that never did love us,
We'll level the proud, and make very degree,
To our royalty bow the knee,
'Tis no less than treason,
'Gainst freedom and reason
For our brethren to be higher than we.

C

First the thing, call'd a king,
To judgment we bring,
And the spawn of the court, that were prouder than he,
And next the two Houses united shall be :
It does to the Roman religion inveigle,
For the state to be two-headed like the spread-eagle ;
  We'll purge the superfluous members away,
  They are too many kings to sway,
      And as we all teach,
      'Tis our liberty's breach,
For the free-born saints to obey.

Not a claw, in the law,
Shall keep us in awe ;
We'll have no cushion-cuffers to tell us of Hell,
For we are all gifted to do it as well :
'Tis freedom that we do hold forth to the nation
To enjoy our fellow-creatures as at the creation ;
  The carnal men's wives are for men of the spirit,
  Their wealth is our own by merit,
      For we that have right,
      By the law called might,
Are the saints that must judge and inherit.

SPECIMENS OF DIURNAL

MONDAY

On Monday both Houses fell into debate,
And were likely to fall by the ears as they sat;
Yet would they not have the business decided,
That they (as the kingdom is) might be divided.
They had an intention to prayers to go,
But extempore prayers are now common too.
To voting they fall; and the key of the work
Was the raising of money for the state and the kirk.
'Tis only free loan: yet this order they make,
That what men would not lend, they should plunder
        and take.
Upon this, the word plunder came into their mind,
And all of them did labour a new one to find:
They call'd it distraining: yet thought it no shame
To persist in the act, which they blush'd for to name.
They voted all persons from Oxford that came,
Should be apprehended: and after the same,
With an humble petition, the king they request
He'd be pleased to return, and be served like the rest.
A message from Oxford, conducing to peace,
Came next to their hands, that armies might cease.
They voted and voted, and still they did vary,

Till at last the whole sense of the house was contrary
To reason; they knew by their arms they might gain
What neither true reason nor law can maintain.
Cessation was voted a dangerous plot;
Because the king would have it, both houses would
     not.
But when they resolv'd, it abroad must be blown,
(To baffle the world) that the king would have none.
And carefully muzzled the mouth of the press,
Lest the truth should peep through their juggling
     dress.
For they knew a cessation would work them more
     harms,
Than Essex could do the cavaliers with his arms.
While they keep the ships and the forts in their hand,
They may be traitors by sea, as well as by land.
The forts will preserve them as long as they stay,
And the ships carry them and their plunder away.
They have therefore good reason to account war the
     better,
For the law will prove to them but a killing letter.

SATURDAY

This day there came news of the taking a ship,
(To see what strange wonders are wrought in the
     deep.)
That a troop of their horse ran into the sea,

And pull'd out a ship alive to the key.
And after much prating and fighting they say,
The ropes serv'd for traces to draw her away.
Sure these were sea-horses, or else by their lying,
They'd make them as famous for swimming as flying.
The rest of the day they spent to bemoan
Their brother the Round-head that to Tyburn was
    gone ;
And could not but think it a barbarous thing,
To hang him for killing a friend to the king.
He was newly baptized, and held it was good
To be washed, yet not in water, but blood.
They ordered for his honour to cut off his ears,
And make him a martyr, but a zealot appears,
And affirm'd him a martyr, for although 'twas his fate
To be hang'd, yet he dy'd for the good of the state.
Then all fell to plotting of matters so deep,
That the silent Speaker fell down fast asleep.
He recovers himself and rubs up his eyes,
Then motions his house that it was time to rise.
So home they went all, and their business referr'd
To the close-committee by them to be heard ;
They took it upon them, but what they did do,
Take notice that none but themselves must know.

ANDREW MARVELL

(Marvell's patriotism and his poetry are both undeniable, but somehow neither shines best when the one enlists the other as a comrade. The matter of his political satires is often insufferably coarse, the manner very often rugged and clumsy. I do not think anything better can be found to represent him than these lines on what was undoubtedly the greatest disgrace of Charles the Second's reign.)

THE DUTCH IN THE MEDWAY

THERE our sick Ships unrigg'd in Summer lay,
Like moulting Fowl, a weak and easy Prey:
For whose strong bulk Earth scarce could Timber
    find,
The Ocean Water, or the Heavens Wind.
Those Oaken Giants of the ancient Race,
That rul'd all Seas, and did our Channel grace.
The conscious Stag, tho' once the Forest's dread,

Flies to the wood, and hides his armless Head :
Ruyter forthwith and Squadron does untack,
They sail securely through the River's track.
And *English* Pilot too (Oh shame ! Oh sin !)
Cheated of's Pay, was he that shew'd them in.
    Our wretched Ships within their Fate attend,
And all our hopes now on frail Chain depend :
(Engine so slight to guard us from the Sea,
It fitter seem'd to Captivate a Flea ;)
A Skipper rude shocks it without respect,
Filling his sails more force to recollect.
Th' *English* from shore the Iron deaf invoke
For its last aid, Hold Chain, or we are broke !
But with her failing weight the *Holland* Keel,
Snapping the brittle Links, does thorough reel,
And to the rest the opening passage shew :
    Monk from the Bank that dismal sight does view.
Our feather'd Gallants which came down that day
To be Spectators safe of the New Play,
Leave him alone when first they hear the Gun,
(*Cornb'ry* the fleetest) and to *London* run.
    Our Seamen whom no dangers shape could fright,
Unpaid, refuse to mount our Ships for spight :
Or to their Fellows Swim on board the *Dutch*,
Who shew the tempting Metal in their clutch.
Oft had he sent, of *Duncomb* and of *Legg*
Cannon and Powder, but in vain, to begg ;
And *Upnor* Castle's ill deserted Wall,

Now needful does for Ammunition call,
He finds, where'er he succour might expect,
Confusion, Folly, Treachery, Fear, Neglect.
    But when the *Royal Charles* (what rage! what
        grief!)
He saw seiz'd, and could give her no relief;
That Sacred Keel that had, as he, restor'd
Its exil'd Sov'reign on its happy board,
And thence the British Admiral became,
Crown'd for that merit with his Master's Name;
That pleasure-boat of War, in whose dear side
Secure, so oft he had this Foe defy'd,
Now a cheap Spoil, and the mean Victor's slave,
Taught the *Dutch* Colours from its Top to wave,
Of former Glories the reproachful thought
With present shame compar'd, his mind distraught.
    Such from *Euphrates* bank a Tigress fell
After her Robbers for her Whelps does yell;
But sees enrag'd the River flow between,
Frustrate Revenge, and Love by loss more keen;
At her own Breast her useless Claws does arm,
She tears herself, 'cause him she cannot harm.
    The Guards plac'd for the Chain's and Fleet's
        defence,
Long since were fled on many a feign'd pretence.
Daniel had there adventur'd, Man of might,
Sweet Painter ! draw his Picture while I write.
    Paint him of person tall, and big of Bone,

Large Limbs like Ox, not to be killed but shown ;
Scarce can burnt Iv'ry feign a hair so black,
Or Face so red, thine Oker and thy Lack,
Mix a vain terror in his Martial look,
And all those lines by which men are mistook ;
But when by shame constrain'd to go on Board,
He heard how the wild Cannon nearer roar'd,
And saw himself confin'd like Sheep in Pen,
Daniel then thought he was in Lions' Den :
But when the frightful Fire-Ships he saw,
Pregnant with Sulphur nearer to him draw,
Captain, Lieutenant, Ensign, all make haste,
E'er in the fiery Furnace they be cast ;
Three Children tall unsing'd, away they row :
Like *Shadrack*, *Mesheck* and *Abednego*.
Each doleful day still with fresh loss returns,
The *Loyal London* now a third time burns.
And the true *Royal Oak*, and *Royal James*,
Ally'd in Fate, increase with theirs her flames.
Of all our Navy none should now survive,
But that the *Ships* themselves were taught to dive ;
And the kind River in its Creek them hides,
Fraughting their pierced Keels with Ouzy sides ;
Up to the Bridge contagious Terror struck,
The *Tow'r* itself with the near danger shook ;
And were not *Ruyter's* Man with ravage cloy'd,
Ev'n *London's* ashes had been then destroy'd ;
Officious fear, however to prevent

Our loss, does so much more our loss augment.
The *Dutch* had robb'd those Jewels of the Crown,
Our Merchant-men, lest they should burn, we drown :
So when the Fire did not enough devour,
The Houses were demolish'd near the Tow'r.
Those *Ships* that yearly from their teaming hole
Unloaded here the Birth of either Pole,
Fir from the North, and Silver from the West,
From the South Perfumes, Spices from the East ;
From *Gambo* Gold, and from the *Ganges* Jems,
Take a short Voyage underneath the *Thames* :
Once a deep River, now with Timber floor'd,
And shrunk, less Navigable, to a Ford.
   Now nothing more at *Chatham's* left to burn,
The *Holland* Squadron leisurely return ;
And spight of *Ruperts* and of *Albermarles*,
To *Ruyter's* Triumph led the Captive *Charles*.
The pleasing sight he often does prolong,
Her Mast erect, tough Cordage, Timber strong,
Her moving shape, all these he doth survey,
And all admires, but most his easy Prey.
The *Seamen* search her all within, without,
Viewing her strength they yet their Conquest doubt ;
Then with rude shouts secure, the Air they vex,
With gamsom joy insulting on her Decks ;
Such the fear'd *Hebrew* Captive, blinded, shorn,
Was led about in sport, the publick scorn.
   Black day accurst ! on thee let no man hale

Out of the Port, or dare to hoyse a Sail,
Or row a Boat in thy unlucky hour, ·
Thee, the Years' Monster, let thy Dam devour;
And constant time to keep his course yet right,
Fill up thy space with a redoubled Night.
When aged *Thames* was bound with Fetters base,
And *Medway* chaste ravisht before his face,
And their dear Off-spring murder'd in their sight,
Thou and thy fellows held'st the odious light.
Sad chance since first that happy Pair was wed,
When all the Rivers grac'd their Nuptial bed,
And Father *Neptune* promis'd to resign
His Empire old to their Immortal line;
Now with vain grief their vainer hopes they rue,
Themselves dishonour'd, and the Gods untrue;
And to each other helpless couple mourn,
As the sad Tortoise for the Sea does groan:
But most they for their darling *Charles* complain,
And were it burnt, yet less would be their pain.
To see that fatal pledge of Sea command,
Now in the Ravisher *de Ruyter's* hand;
The *Thames* roar'd, swooning *Medway* turned her
     tyde,
And were they mortal, both for grief had dy'd.
    The Court in Fathering yet it self doth please,
And female *Steward* there rules the four Seas,
But fate does still accumulate our woes,
And *Richmond* her commands, as Ruyter those.

After this loss, to relish discontent,
Some one must be accus'd by punishment;
All our Miscarriages on *Pett* must fall,
His name alone seems fit to answer all.
Whose counsel first did this mad War beget?
Who all Commands sold through the Navy?   *Pett.*
Who would not follow when the *Dutch* were beat?
Who treated out the Time at *Bergen*?   *Pett.*
Who the *Dutch* Fleet with storms disabled met?
And rifling Prizes them neglected?   *Pett.*
Who with false News prevented the Gazette?
The Fleet divided, writ for *Rupert*?   *Pett.*
Who all our Seamen cheated of their debt,
And all our Prizes who did swallow?   *Pett.*
Who did advise no Navy out to Set?
And who the Forts left unprepared?   *Pett.*
Who to supply with Powder did forget
Languard, Sheerness, Gravesend and *Upnor*?   *Pett.*
Who all our Ships exposed in *Chattham* Nett?
Who should it be but the Fanatick *Pett*?
Pett, the Sea-architect in making *Ships*,
Was the first cause of all these Naval slips.
Had he not built, none of these faults had been;
If no Creation, there had been no sin;
But his great Crime, one Boat away he sent,
That lost our Fleet, and did our flight prevent.

JOHN DRYDEN

(It seemed superfluous to draw on Absalom and Achitophel, *the greatest of Dryden's political poems. His political prologues and epilogues are defaced both by coarseness and ferocity.* The Medal *is less generally known than it ought to be, and though the personal satire is less lively than in* Absalom and Achitophel, *the political argument is thorough; and the extraordinary aptitude of Glorious John's muse for reasoning in verse is nowhere better shown. There is an interesting and not improbable story that Charles the Second himself suggested the subject, and even the treatment, to the poet; I say not improbable, for Charles's ability is unquestionable, and it was Dryden's way to work better on a suggestion or a pattern than quite independently.)*

THE MEDAL

A SATIRE AGAINST SEDITION

OF all our antic sights and pageantry
Which English idiots run in crowds to see,

The Polish Medal bears the prize alone ;
A monster, more the favourite of the town
Than either fairs or theatres have shown.
Never did art so well with nature strive,
Nor ever idol seemed so much alive ;
So like the man, so golden to the sight,
So base within, so counterfeit and light.
One side is filled with title and with face ;
And, lest the king should want a regal place,
On the reverse a tower the town surveys,
O'er which our mounting sun his beams displays.
The word, pronounced aloud by shrieval voice,
Lætamur, which in Polish is *Rejoice*,
The day, month, year, to the great act are joined,
And a new canting holiday designed.
Five days he sate for every cast and look,
Four more than God to finish Adam took.
But who can tell what essence angels are
Or how long Heaven was making Lucifer ?
Oh, could the style that copied every grace
And ploughed such furrows for an eunuch face,
Could it have formed his ever-changing will,
The various piece had tired the graver's skill !
A martial hero first, with early care
Blown, like a pigmy by the winds, to war ;
A beardless chief, a rebel ere a man,
So young his hatred to his Prince began.
Next this, (how wildly will ambition steer !)

A vermin wriggling in the usurper's ear,
Bartering his venal wit for sums of gold,
He cast himself into the saint-like mould;
Groaned, sighed, and prayed, while godliness was gain,
The loudest bag-pipe of the squeaking train.
But, as 'tis hard to cheat a juggler's eyes,
His open lewdness he could ne'er disguise.
There split the saint; for hypocritic zeal
Allows no sins but those it can conceal.
Whoring to scandal gives too large a scope;
Saints must not trade, but they may interlope.
The ungodly principle was all the same;
But a gross cheat betrays his partner's game.
Besides, their pace was formal, grave, and slack;
His nimble wit outran the heavy pack.
Yet still he found his fortune at a stay,
Whole droves of blockheads choking up his way;
They took, but not rewarded, his advice;
Villain and wit exact a double price.
Power was his aim; but thrown from that pretence,
The wretch turned loyal in his own defence,
And malice reconciled him to his Prince.
Him in the anguish of his soul he served,
Rewarded faster still than he deserved.
Behold him now exalted into trust,
His counsels oft convenient, seldom just;
Even in the most sincere advice he gave
He had a grudging still to be a knave.

The frauds he learnt in his fanatic years
Made him uneasy in his lawful gears.
At best, as little honest as he could,
And, like white witches, mischievously good.
To his first bias longingly he leans
And rather would be great by wicked means.
Thus framed for ill, he loosed our triple hold,
(Advice unsafe, precipitous, and bold.)
From hence those tears, that Ilium of our woe :
Who helps a powerful friend forearms a foe.
What wonder if the waves prevail so far,
When he cut down the banks that made the bar ?
Seas follow but their nature to invade ;
But he by art our native strength betrayed.
So Samson to his foe his force confest,
And to be shorn lay slumbering on her breast.
But when this fatal counsel, found too late,
Exposed its author to the public hate,
When his just sovereign by no impious way
Could be seduced to arbitrary sway,
Forsaken of that hope, he shifts his sail,
Drives down the current with a popular gale,
And shows the fiend confessed without a veil.
He preaches to the crowd that power is lent,
But not conveyed to kingly government,
That claims successive bear no binding force,
That coronation oaths are things of course ;
Maintains the multitude can never err,

And sets the people in the papal chair.
The reason's obvious, *interest never lies*;
The most have still their interest in their eyes,
The power is always theirs, and power is ever wise.
Almighty crowd! thou shortenest all dispute,
Power is thy essence, wit thy attribute!
Nor faith nor reason make thee at a stay,
Thou leapst o'er all eternal truths in thy Pindaric way!
Athens, no doubt, did righteously decide,
When Phocion and when Socrates were tried;
As righteously they did those dooms repent;
Still they were wise, whatever way they went.
Crowds err not, though to both extremes they run:
To kill the father and recall the son.
Some think the fools were most, as times went then
But now the world's o'erstocked with prudent men.
The common cry is even religion's test;
The Turk's is at Constantinople best,
Idols in India, Popery at Rome,
And our own worship only true at home,
And true but for the time; 'tis hard to know
How long we please it shall continue so;
This side to-day, and that to-morrow burns;
So all are God Almighties in their turns.
A tempting doctrine, plausible and new;
What fools our fathers were, if this be true!
Who, to destroy the seeds of civil war,
Inherent right in monarchs did declare;

D

And, that a lawful power might never cease,
Secured succession to secure our peace.
Thus property and sovereign sway at last
In equal balances were justly cast;
But this new Jehu spurs the hot-mouthed horse,
Instructs the beast to know his native force,
To take the bit between his teeth and fly
To the next headlong steep of anarchy.
Too happy England, if our good we knew,
Would we possess the freedom we pursue!
The lavish government can give no more;
Yet we repine, and plenty makes us poor.
God tried us once; our rebel fathers fought;
He glutted them with all the power they sought,
Till, mastered by their own usurping brave,
The free-born subject sunk into a slave.
We loathe our manna, and we long for quails;
Ah! what is man, when his own wish prevails!
How rash, how swift to plunge himself in ill,
Proud of his power and boundless in his will!
That kings can do no wrong we must believe;
None can they do, and must they all receive?
Help, Heaven, or sadly we shall see an hour
When neither wrong nor right are in their power!
Already they have lost their best defence,
The benefit of laws which they dispense.
No justice to their righteous cause allowed,
But baffled by an arbitrary crowd;

And medals graved, their conquest to record,
The stamp and coin of their adopted lord.

    *   *   *   *   *

But thou, the pander of the people's hearts,
(O crooked soul and serpentine in arts !)
Whose blandishments a loyal land have whored,
And broke the bonds she plighted to her lord,
What curses on thy blasted name will fall,
Which age to age their legacy shall call,
For all must curse the woes that must descend on all!
Religion thou hast none : thy mercury
Has passed through every sect, or theirs through thee.
But what thou givest, that venom still remains,
And the poxed nation feels thee in their brains.
What else inspires the tongues and swells the breasts
Of all thy bellowing renegado priests,
That preach up thee for God, dispense thy laws,
And with thy stum ferment their fainting cause,
Fresh fumes of madness raise, and toil and sweat,
To make the formidable cripple great ?
Yet should thy crimes succeed, should lawless power
Compass those ends thy greedy hopes devour,
Thy canting friends thy mortal foes would be,
Thy god and theirs will never long agree ;
For thine, if thou hast any, must be one
That lets the world and human kind alone ;
A jolly god that passes hours too well
To promise Heaven or threaten us with Hell,

That unconcerned can at rebellion sit
And wink at crimes he did himself commit.
A tyrant theirs ; the heaven their priesthood paints
A conventicle of gloomy sullen saints ;
A heaven, like Bedlam, slovenly and sad,
Foredoomed for souls with false religion mad.
    Without a vision poets can foreshow
What all but fools by common sense may know :
If true succession from our Isle should fail,
And crowds profane with impious arms prevail,
Not thou nor those thy factious arts engage
Shall reap that harvest of rebellious rage,
With which thou flatterest thy decrepit age.
The swelling poison of the several sects,
Which, wanting vent, the nation's health infects,
Shall burst its bag ; and fighting out their way,
The various venoms on each other prey.
The Presbyter, puffed up with spiritual pride,
Shall on the necks of the lewd nobles ride,
His brethren damn, the civil power defy,
And parcel out republic prelacy.
But short shall be his reign ; his rigid yoke
And tyrant power will puny sects provoke,
And frogs, and toads, and all the tadpole train
Will croak to Heaven for help from this devouring
    crane.
The cut-throat sword and clamorous gown shall jar
In sharing their ill-gotten spoils of war ;

Chiefs shall be grudged the part which they pretend ;
Lords envy lords, and friends with every friend
About their impious merit shall contend.
The surly Commons shall respect deny
And justle peerage out with property.
Their General either shall his trust betray
And force the crowd to arbitrary sway,
Or they, suspecting his ambitious aim,
In hate of kings shall cast anew the frame,
And thrust out Collatine that bore their name.

Thus inborn broils the factions would engage,
Or wars of exiled heirs, or foreign rage,
Till halting vengeance overtook our age,
And our wild labours, wearied into rest,
Reclined us on a rightful monarch's breast.

ROCHESTER

(What was said above of Marvell applies with treble force to Rochester.   Most of his longer political satires are simply filthy lampoons on Charles and his mistresses.   But these two epigrams—one universally, the other generally known—are among the best of their kind.)

EPITAPH ON KING CHARLES II.

HERE lies our Sovereign Lord the King
    Whose word no man relies on.
Who never said a foolish thing
    And never did a wise one.

THE COMMONS PETITION TO THE KING

In all Humility we crave
Our Sovereign may be our Slave,
And humbly beg that he may be
Betray'd to us most loyally ;
And if he pleases to lay down
His Scepter, Dignity, and Crown,
We'll make him for the time to come
The greatest Prince in *Christendom*.

THE KING'S ANSWER

Charles at this Time having no need,
Thanks you as much as if he did.

THE 'STATE POEMS'

(The great collection called the State Poems *(many of which have nothing to do with politics) contains a vast deal of rubbish and some things of value. I have extracted from it the very pointed and excellent* Young Statesmen, *which is in the original attributed to Dryden, but without evidence, nor do I think the sentiments are his. The* Epigram on Somers *is neat if rather too complimentary. The Jacobite satire on the successors of the nonjuring bishops has more vigour, more polish, and less indecency than almost any of its kind. The* Williamite Curse *which follows is much better than usually came from that party as literature ; and not more savage as sentiment than most of the sentiment on both sides.* Lilliburlero *is no doubt sad doggerel, but it had such vogue and influence, and is so much more often referred to than given even in part by historians, that I thought it might find a place.)*

ON THE YOUNG STATESMEN

I

Clarendon had Law and Sense,
  Clifford was Fierce and Brave,
Bennet's grave Look was a Pretence,
And *D——y's* matchless Impudence
  Help'd to support the knave.

2

But *Sund——d, God——n, L——y,*
These will appear such Chits in story,
  'Twill turn all Politicks to Jests,
To be repeated like *John Dory,*
  When Fidlers sing at Feasts.

3

Protect us, mighty Providence,
  What wou'd these Madmen have?
First, they wou'd bribe us without Pence,
Deceive us without common Sense,
  And without Pow'r enslave.

4

Shall Free-born Men in humble awe,
     Submit to servile shame ;
Who from Content and Custom, draw
The same Right to be ruled by Law
     Which Kings pretend to Reign ?

5

The Duke shall wield his conq'ring Sword,
     The Chancellor make his Speech ;
The King shall pass his honest Word,
The pawn'd Revenue Sums afford ;
     And then come kiss my Breech.

6

· So I have seen a King on Chess
     (His Rooks and Knights withdrawn,
His Queen and Bishops in distress)
Shifting about, grow less and less,
     With here and there a pawn.

ON SOME VOTES AGAINST THE LORD
SOMERS

WHEN Envy does at *Athens* rise,
     And swells the Town with murmurs loud,

Not *Aristides*, Just and Wise,
  Can scape the moody factious Crowd.

Each Vote augments the common Cry,
  While he that holds the fatal Shell,
Can give no Cause, or Reason why,
  But being Great, and doing Well.

ON THE PROMOTED BISHOPS

I

For the Miracles done
This Year Ninety One,
Let's go forth and Proclaim a Thanksgiving;
  Late Archbishop we sing
  To the Tune of Late King,
While *J*—— and Old *S*——*ft* are Living.

2

Of this Protestant Land
The Fleet not half Mann'd,
Is a Miracle scarce worth our Trouble:
  We judge of the Weight
  Of this Politick State,
Now the Church and the Throne carry double.

3

The Law now in force
Made a solemn Divorce
Between J—— C—— and his Church has ;
'Twill a Miracle show,
As the Blessed Times go,
If Religion proves worth a Year's Purchase.

4

The Gospel now thrives,
For our Lord hath two Wives,
And a Prelate his See of each Party :
That the Law doth respect
The new B——ps Elect
Or the new second Wife of *Clancarty*.

5

As to the Pastoral Staff,
We at *T——n* laugh,
And the Projects of dull Politicians ;
Spite of all Satan's Power
Aaron's Rod shall devour
The Rod of their Heathen Magicians

6

Our Impotent Fleet
Our starv'd Army may greet,
And at each others Confidence wonder ;
With an Army unpaid,
And a Navy betray'd,
We fast to keep great *Lewis* under.

7

As old *Babylon* saith,
The Protestant Faith
Took deep Root from the Codpiece of *Harry* ;
We good Witness can bring,
The good Bishops all Spring
From the conducts of *W——* and *M——*.

CURSE

CURS'D be the Stars which did Ordain
Queen Bess a Maiden-Life should Reign ;
Married she might have brought an Heir,
Nor had we known a *S——t* here.
Curs'd be the Tribe who at *Whitehall*

Slew one o' th Name, and slew not all.
Curs'd be the Second, who took Gold
From *France*, and *Britain's* Honour Sold :
But Curs'd of all be J——— the last,
The worst of Kings, of Fools the best,
And doubly Cursed be those Knaves,
Who out of Loyalty would make us Slaves,
Curs'd be the Clergy who desire   ⎫
The *French* to bring in *James* the Squire, ⎬
And save your Church so as by Fire.   ⎭

 Curst be the Earl of *T*———*ton.*
Who almost had three Lands undone ;
Who out of Fear, of Pride, or Gain,
Betray'd our Land, and lost her Main.

 Curs'd be the Ministers of State,
Who keep our Fleet till 'tis too late ;
Who have Six Weeks the Cause disputed,
When the whole in two might have recruited.

 Curs'd be the name of *Englishman,*
To Curse it more, live *T*———*ton.*
Let Resolution only be
King *William's* noble Property :
He hath done what we ne'er could do, ⎫
Ill to himself, to us been true.   ⎬
Prove that among us, and curse me too. ⎭

SONG

Ho, Brother *Teague*, dost hear de Decree?
  Lilli Burlero Bullena-la.
Dat we shall have a new Debity,
  Lilli Burlero Bullena-la.
  Lero lero, Lero lero, lilliburlero bullena-la,
  Lero lero, etc.

Ho by my Shoul it is a troat,
  Lilli burlero, etc.
And he will cut all de *English* Throat,
  Lilli, etc.
  Lero lero, etc.
  Lero lero, etc.

Tho' by my Shoul de *English* do praat,
  Lilli burlero, etc.
De Laws on dare side, and Creish know what,
  Lilli, etc.
  Lero lero, etc.
  Lero lero, etc.

But if Dispence do come from de Pope,
  Lilli burlero, etc.

We'll hang *Magna Charta*, and demselves in a
    Rope,
    Lilli, etc.
  Lero lero, etc.
  Lero lero, etc.

And de Good *Talbot* is made a Lord,
    Lilli burlero, etc.
And he with brave Lads is coming aboard,
    Lilli, etc.
  Lero lero, etc.
  Lero lero, etc.

Who aul in *France* have tauken a Sware,
    Lilli burlero, etc.
Dat dey will have no Protestant here,
    Lilli, etc.
  Lero lero, etc.
  Lero lero, etc.

O, But why does he stay behind ?
    Lilli burlero, etc.
Ho, by my Shoul, 'tis a Protestant Wind,
    Lilli, etc.
  Lero lero, etc.
  Lero lero, etc.

Now *Tyrconnel* is come ashore,
    Lilli burlero, etc.
And we shall have Commissions gillore,
    Lilli, etc.
  Lero lero, etc.
  Lero lero, etc.

And he dat will not go to Mass,
    Lilli burlero, etc.
Shall turn out and look like an Ass,
    Lilli, etc.
  Lero lero, etc.
  Lero lero, etc.

Now, now de Hereticks all go down,
    Lilli burlero, etc.
By Creish and St. *Patrick* the Nation's our own,
    Lilli, etc.
  Lero lero, etc.
  Lero lero, etc.

THE SECOND PART

By Creish, my dear *Morish*, vat maukes de sho
    shad?
    Lilli burlero, etc.
De Hereticks jeer us, and mauke me mad,

E

    Lilli, etc.
  Lero lero, etc.
  Lero lero, etc.

Pox tauke me, dear Teague, but I am in a Raage,
    Lilli burlero, etc.
Poo-oo, what Impudence is in dis Aage !
    Lilli, etc.
  Lero lero, etc.
  Lero lero, etc.

Dey shay dat *Tyrconnel's* a Friend to de Mash,
    Lilli burlero, etc.
For which he's a Traytor, a Pimp, and an Ass,
    Lilli, etc.
  Lero lero, etc.
  Lero lero, etc.

Ara ! Plague tauke me now, I mauke a Sware,
    Lilli burlero, etc.
I to Shaint *Tyburn* will mauke a great Pray'r,
    Lilli, etc.
  Lero lero, etc.
  Lero lero, etc.

O, I will pray to Shaint *Patrick's* Frock,
    Lilli burlero, etc.

Or to *Loretto's* Sacred Smock,
   Lilli, etc.
  Lero lero, etc.
  Lero lero, etc.

Now, a Pox tauke me, what dost dow tink?
   Lilli burlero, etc.
De *English* Confusion tò Popery drink,
   Lilli, etc.
  Lero lero, etc.
  Lero lero, etc.

And by my Shoul de Mash-house pull down,
   Lilli burlero, etc.
While dey were swaaring de Mayor of de Town,
   Lilli, etc.
  Lero lero, etc.
  Lero lero, etc.

O Fait and be! I'll make a Decree,
   Lilli burlero, etc.
And swaare by the Chancellor's Modesty,
   Lilli, etc.
  Lero lero, etc.
  Lero lero, etc.

Dat I no longer in *English* will stay
   Lilli burlero, etc.

For by Gode dey will hang us out of the way,
        Lilli, etc.
    Lero lero, etc.
    Lero lero, etc.

Vat if the *Dush* should come as dey hope,
        Lilli burlero, etc.
To up hang us for all de Dispense of de Pope.
        Lilli, etc.
    Lero lero, etc.
    Lero lero, etc.

DANIEL DEFOE

(The merit of The True-Born Englishman *lies wholly in the matter ; but that matter was effective at the time, and the sketch of the English character here given is at least the work of a shrewd observer—a typical English-man himself in many ways, and, when it suited him, an uncompromising writer.)*

CHARACTER OF ENGLISHMEN

In their religion, they're so uneven,
That each man goes his own byway to heaven.
Tenacious of mistakes to that degree,
That ev'ry man pursues it sep'rately,
And fancies none can find the way but he :
So shy of one another they are grown,
As if they strove to get to heaven alone.
Rigid and zealous, positive and grave,
And ev'ry grace, but charity, they have ;

This makes them so ill-natured and uncivil,
That all men think an Englishman the devil.

SURLY to strangers, froward to their friend,
Submit to love with a reluctant mind,
Resolved to be ungrateful and unkind.
If, by necessity, reduced to ask,
The giver has the difficultest task :
For what's bestow'd they awkwardly receive,
And always take less freely than they give ;
The obligation is their highest grief,
They never love where they accept relief ;
So sullen in their sorrows, that 'tis known
They'll rather die than their afflictions own ;
And if relieved, it is too often true,
That they'll abuse their benefactors too ;
For in distress their haughty stomach's such,
They hate to see themselves obliged too much ;
Seldom contented, often in the wrong,
Hard to be pleased at all, and never long.

IF your mistakes their ill opinion gain,
No merit can their favour re-obtain :
And if they're not vindictive in their fury,
'Tis their inconstant temper does secure ye :
Their brain's so cool, their passion seldom burns ;
For all's condensed before the flame returns :
The fermentation's of so weak a matter,

The humid damps the flame, and runs it all to water :
So though the inclination may be strong,
They're pleased by fits, and never angry long :

THEN, if good-nature show some slender proof,
They never think they have reward enough ;
But, like our modern Quakers of the town,
Expect your manners, and return you none.

FRIENDSHIP, th' abstracted union of the mind,
Which all men seek, but very few can find ;
Of all the nations in the universe,
None talk on't more, or understand it less ; '
For if it does their property annoy,
Their property their friendship will destroy.
As you discourse them, you shall hear them tell
All things in which they think they do excel :
No panegyric needs their praise record,
An Englishman ne'er wants his own good word.
His first discourses gen'rally appear,
Prologued with his own wond'rous character :
When, to illustrate his own good name,
He never fails his neighbour to defame.
And yet he really designs no wrong,
His malice goes no further than his tongue.
But, pleased to tattle, he delights to rail,
To satisfy the letch'ry of a tale.
His own dear praises close the ample speech,

Tells you how wise he is, that is, how rich :
For wealth is wisdom ; he that's rich is wise ;
And all men learned poverty despise :
His generosity comes next, and then
Concludes, that he's a true-born Englishman ;
And they, 'tis known, are generous and free,
Forgetting, and forgiving injury :
Which may be true, thus rightly understood,
Forgiving ill turns, and forgetting good.

CHEERFUL in labour when they've undertook it,
But out of humour, when they're out of pocket.
But if their belly and their pocket's full,
They may be phlegmatic, but never dull :
And if a bottle does their brains refine,
It makes their wit as sparkling as their wine.

As for the general vices which we find,
They're guilty of in common with mankind,
Satire forbear, and silently endure,
We must conceal the crimes we cannot cure ;
Nor shall my verse the brighter sex defame,
For English beauty will preserve her name ;
Beyond dispute agreeable and fair,
And modester than other nations are ;
For where the vice prevails, the great temptation
Is want of money more than inclination ;

In general this only is allow'd,
They're something noisy, and a little proud.

AN Englishman is gentlest in command,
Obedience is a stranger in the land:
Hardly subjected to the magistrate;
For Englishmen do all subjection hate.
Humblest when rich, but peevish when they're poor,
And think whate'er they have, they merit more.

THE meanest English plowman studies law,
And keeps thereby the magistrates in awe,
Will boldly tell them what they ought to do,
And sometimes punish their omissions too.

THEIR liberty and property's so dear,
They scorn their laws or governors to fear;
So bugbear'd with the name of slavery,
They can't submit to their own liberty.
Restraint from ill is freedom to the wise!
But Englishmen do all restraint despise.
Slaves to the liquor, drudges to the pots;
The mob are statesmen, and their statesmen sots.

THEIR governors, they count such dang'rous things,
That 'tis their custom to affront their kings:
So jealous of the power their kings possess'd,

Daniel Defoe

They suffer neither power nor kings to rest.
The bad with force they eagerly subdue ;
The good with constant clamours they pursue,
And did King Jesus reign, they'd murmur too.
A discontented nation, and by far
Harder to rule in times of peace than war :
Easily set together by the ears,
And full of causeless jealousies and fears :
Apt to revolt, and willing to rebel,
And never are contented when they're well.
No government could ever please them long,
Could tie their hands, or rectify their tongue.
In this, to ancient Israel well compared,
Eternal murmurs are among them heard.

It was but lately, that they were oppress'd,
Their rights invaded, and their laws suppress'd :
When nicely tender of their liberty,
Lord ! what a noise they made of slavery.
In daily tumults show'd their discontent,
Lampoon'd their king, and mock'd his government.
And if in arms they did not first appear,
'Twas want of force, and not for want of fear.
In humbler tone than English used to do,
At foreign hands for foreign aid they sue.

William, the great successor of Nassau,
Their prayers heard, and their oppressions saw ;

He saw and saved them : God and him they praised
To this their thanks, to that their trophies raised.
But glutted with their own felicities,
They soon their new deliverer despise ;
Say all their prayers back, their joy disown,
Unsing their thanks, and pull their trophies down :
Their harps of praise are on the willows hung ;
For Englishmen are ne'er contented long.

MATTHEW PRIOR, JONATHAN SWIFT, RICHARD GLOVER, ETC.

(Prior's political verse is, as a whole, disappointing and the author was perhaps as much too frivolous as Swift was too earnest for the due composition of the kind. I have therefore drawn but sparingly on both. Admiral Hosier's Ghost, a poor thing, but with a certain smoothness, was very famous and effective in its day. I add one or two minor things of the early Georgian time.)

MATTHEW PRIOR

WRITTEN IN THE BEGINNING OF MÉZERAY'S HISTORY OF FRANCE

WHATE'ER thy countrymen have done,
By law and wit, by sword and gun,
   In thee is faithfully recited :

And all the living world that view
Thy work, give thee the praises due,
　At once instructed and delighted.

Yet, for the fame of all these deeds,
What beggar in the Invalids,
　With lameness broke, with blindness smitten,
Wish'd ever decently to die,
To have been either Mézeray,
　Or any monarch he has written.

It's strange, dear author, yet it true is,
That, down from Pharamond to Louis,
　All covet life, yet call it pain ;
All feel the ill, yet shun the cure :
Can sense this paradox endure ?
　Resolve me, Cambray or Fontaine.

The man in graver tragic known,
(Though his best part long since was done)
　Still on the stage desires to tarry :
And he who play'd the Harlequin,
After the jest still loads the scene,
　Unwilling to retire though weary.

A PARAPHRASE FROM THE FRENCH

IN grey-hair'd Celia's wither'd arms
    As mighty Lewis lay,
She cry'd, ' If I have any charms,
    My dearest, let's away !
For you, my love, is all my fear,
    Hark how the drums do rattle ;
Alas, sir ! what should you do here
    In dreadful day of battle ?
Let little Orange stay and fight,
    For danger's his diversion ;
The wise will think you in the right,
    Not to expose your person :
Nor vex your thoughts how to repair
    The ruins of your glory :
You ought to leave so mean a care
    To those who pen your story.
Are not Boileau and Corneille paid
    For panegyric writing ?
They know how heroes may be made,
    Without the help of fighting.
When foes too saucily approach,
    'Tis best to leave them fairly ;
Put six good horses in your coach,
    And carry me to Marly.

Let Bouflers, to secure your fame,
 Go take some town, or buy it ;
Whilst you, great sir, at Nostre dame,
 Te Deum sing in quiet !'

JONATHAN SWIFT

ON THE IRISH CLUB

YE paltry underlings of state ;
Ye senators who love to prate ;
Ye rascals of inferior note,
Who for a dinner sell a vote ;
Ye pack of pensionary peers,
Whose fingers itch for poets' ears ;
Ye bishops far removed from saints ;
Why all this rage ?   Why these complaints ?
Why against printers all this noise ?
This summoning of blackguard boys ?
Why so sagacious in your guesses ?
Your *effs*, and *tees*, and *arrs*, and *esses* ?
Take my advice ; to make you safe,
I know a shorter way by half.
The point is plain : remove the cause ;
Defend your liberties and laws.
Be sometimes to your country true,

Have once the public good in view :
Bravely despise champagne at court,
And choose to dine at home with port :
Let prelates, by their good behaviour,
Convince us they believe a Saviour ;
Nor sell what they so dearly bought,
This country, now their own, for nought.
Ne'er did a true satiric Muse
Virtue or innocence abuse ;
And 'tis against poetic rules
To rail at men by nature fools :
But * * * * * * * * *
* * * * * * * * * *

RICHARD GLOVER

ADMIRAL HOSIER'S GHOST

As near Porto-Bello lying
    On the gently swelling flood,
At midnight with streamers flying,
    Our triumphant navy rode ;
There while Vernon sat all-glorious
    From the Spaniard's late defeat ;
And his crews, with shouts victorious,
    Drank success to England's fleet :

On a sudden shrilly sounding,
 Hideous yells and shrieks were heard :
Then each heart with fear confounding,
 A sad troop of ghosts appear'd,
All in dreary hammocs shrouded,
 Which for winding-sheets they wore,
And with looks by sorrow clouded,
 Frowning on that hostile shore.

On them gleamed the Moon's wan lustre,
 When the shade of Hosier brave
His pale bands was seen to muster,
 Rising from their wat'ry grave :
O'er the glimm'ring wave he hy'd him
 Where the Burford rear'd her sail,
With three thousand ghosts beside him,
 And in groans did Vernon hail.

' Heed, O heed, our fatal story,
 I am Hosier's injur'd ghost,
You, who now have purchas'd glory
 At this place where I was lost,
Though in Porto-Bello's ruin
 You now triumph free from fears,
When you think on our undoing,
 You will mix your joy with tears.

F

'See these mournful spectres, sweeping
Ghastly o'er this hated wave,
Whose wan cheeks are stain'd with weeping;
These were English captains brave:
Mark those numbers pale and horrid,
Those were once my sailors bold,
Lo! each hangs his drooping forehead,
While his dismal tale is told.

'I, by twenty sail attended,
Did this Spanish town affright:
Nothing then its wealth defended
But my orders not to fight:
O! that in this rolling ocean
I had cast them in disdain,
And obeyed my heart's warm motion,
To have quell'd the pride of Spain.

'For resistance I could fear none,
But with twenty ships had done
What thou, brave and happy Vernon,
Hast achiev'd with six alone.
Then the Bastimentos never
Had our foul dishonour seen,
Nor the sea the sad receiver
Of this gallant train had been.

' Thus, like thee, proud Spain dismaying,
 And her galleons leading home,
Though condemn'd for disobeying,
 I had met a traitor's doom ;
To have fall'n, my country crying
 He has play'd an English part,
Had been better far than dying
 Of a griev'd and broken heart.

' Unrepining at thy glory,
 Thy successful arms we hail ;
But remember our sad story,
 And let Hosier's wrongs prevail.
Sent in this foul clime to languish
 Think what thousands fell in vain,
Wasted with disease and anguish,
 Not in glorious battle slain.

' Hence, with all my train attending
 From their oozy tombs below,
Through the hoary foam ascending,
 Here I feed my constant woe :
Here the Bastimentos viewing,
 We recall our shameful doom,
And our plaintive cries renewing,
 Wander through the midnight gloom.

' O'er these waves for ever mourning
    Shall we roam depriv'd of rest,
If to Britain's shores returning,
    You neglect my just request.
After this proud foe subduing,
    When your patriot friends you see,
Think on vengeance for my ruin,
    And for England sham'd in me.'

(ANON.) EPITAPH ON PRINCE FREDERICK

HERE lies Fred,
Who was alive and is dead.
Had it been his father,
I had much rather :
Had it been his brother,
Still better than another :
Had it been his sister
No one would have missed her :
Had it been the whole generation,
So much the better for the nation ;
But since 'tis only Fred,
Who was alive and is dead,
Why there's no more to be said.

MARK AKENSIDE

(While several of the second-rate poets of the eighteenth century have recently had justice, or more than justice, done to them, Akenside has, I think, rather missed his due. There is a certain unreality about his general style, and with Johnson making fun of his political attitude on one side, and Macaulay on the other, it may seem Quixotic to defend it. But the Epistle to Curio, *which the bard altered into an unreadable* Ode to Curio, *has always been admired traditionally, and I myself have a very warm and sincere admiration for it. It seems to me among the very greatest achievements in the style of Pope—an artificial thing that is really and almost sincerely artful. The motive of course was that ' Curio,' i.e. Pulteney, after giving himself the extremest patriotic airs during the great Walpolian battle, settled very comfortably into peerages and pensions when Walpole was ousted.)*

AN EPISTLE TO CURIO

THRICE has the Spring beheld thy faded fame,
And the fourth Winter rises on thy shame,
Since I exulting grasp'd the votive shell,
In sounds of triumph all thy praise to tell ;
Blest could my skill through ages make thee shine,
And proud to mix my memory with thine.
But now the cause that wak'd my song before,
With praise, with triumph, crowns the toil no more.
If to the glorious man, whose faithful cares,
Nor quell'd by malice, nor relax'd by years,
Had aw'd Ambition's wild audacious hate,
And dragg'd at length Corruption to her fate ;
If every tongue its large applauses ow'd
And well-earn'd laurels every Muse bestow'd ;
If public Justice urg'd the high reward,
And Freedom smil'd on the devoted bard :
Say then, to him whose levity or lust
Laid all a people's generous hopes in dust ;
Who taught Ambition firmer heights of power,
And sav'd Corruption at her hopeless hour ;
Does not each tongue its execrations owe ?
Shall not each Muse a wreath of shame bestow ?
And public Justice sanctify the award ?
And Freedom's hand protect th' impartial bard ?

Yet long reluctant I forbore thy name,
Long watch'd thy virtue like a dying flame,
Hung o'er each glimmering spark with anxious eyes,
And wish'd and hop'd the light again would rise.
But since thy guilt still more entire appears,
Since no art hides, no supposition clears ;
Since vengeful Slander now too sinks her blast,
And the first rage of party-haste is past ;
Calm as the Judge of Truth, at length I come
To weigh thy merits and pronounce thy doom :
So may my trust from all reproach be free,
And Earth and Time confirm the fair decree.
   There are who say they view'd without amaze
Thy sad reverse of all thy former praise ;
That through the pageants of a patriot's name,
They pierc'd the foulness of thy secret aim ;
Or deem'd thy arm exalted but to throw
The public thunder on a private foe.
But I, whose soul consented to thy cause,
Who felt thy genius stamp its own applause,
Who saw the spirits of each glorious age
Move in thy bosom, and direct thy rage ;
I scorn'd the ungenerous gloss of slavish minds,
The owl-ey'd race, whom Virtue's lustre blinds.
Spite of the learned in the ways of Vice,
And all who prove that each man has his price,
I still believ'd thy end was just and free ;
And yet, even yet believe it—spite of thee.

Even though thy mouth impure has dar'd disclaim,
Urg'd by the wretched impotence of shame,
Whatever filial cares thy zeal had paid
To laws infirm and liberty decay'd ;
Has begg'd Ambition to forgive the show ;
Has told Corruption thou wert ne'er her foe ;
Has boasted in thy country's awful ear,
Her gross delusion when she held thee dear ;
How tame she followed thy tempestuous call,
And heard thy pompous tales, and trusted all—
Rise from your sad abodes, ye curst of old
For laws subverted, and for cities sold !
Paint all the noblest trophies of your guilt,
The oaths you perjur'd and the blood you spilt ;
Yet must you one untempted vileness own,
One dreadful palm reserv'd for him alone :
With studied arts his country's praise to spurn,
To beg the infamy he did not earn,
To challenge hate when honour was his due,
And plead his crimes where all his virtue knew.
Do robes of state the guarded heart enclose
From each fair feeling human nature knows ?
Can pompous titles stun the enchanted ear
To all that reason, all that sense, would hear ?
Else could thou e'er desert thy sacred post,
In such unthankful baseness to be lost ?
Else could'st thou wed the emptiness of vice,
And yield thy glories at an idiot's price ?

When they who, loud for liberty and laws,
In doubtful times had fought their country's cause,
When now of conquest and dominion sure,
They sought alone to hold their fruits secure ;
When taught by these, Oppression hid the face
To leave Corruption stronger in her place,
By silent spells to work the public fate,
And taint the vitals of the passive state,
Till healing Wisdom should avail no more,
And Freedom loathe to tread the poisoned shore ;
Then, like some guardian god that flies to save
The weary pilgrim from an instant grave,
Whom, sleeping and secure, the guileful snake
Steals near and nearer through the peaceful brake ;
Then Curio rose to ward the public woe,
To wake the heedless, and incite the slow,
Against Corruption, Liberty to arm,
And quell the enchantress by a mightier charm.
    Swift o'er the land the fair contagion flew,
And with the country's hopes thy honours grew.
Thee, patriot, the patrician roof confess'd :
Thy powerful voice the rescued merchant bless'd ;
Of thee with awe the rural hearth resounds ;
The bowl to thee the grateful sailor crowns ;
Touch'd in the sighing shade with manlier fires,
To trace thy step the love-sick youth aspires ;
The learn'd recluse, who oft amaz'd had read
Of Grecian heroes, Roman patriots dead,

With new amazement hears a living name
Pretend to share in such forgotten fame;
And he who scorning courts and courtly ways,
Left the tame track of these dejected days,
The life of nobler ages to renew
In virtues sacred from a monarch's view,
Rous'd by thy labours from the blest retreat,
Where social ease and public passions meet,
Again ascending treads the civil scene,
To act and be a man, as thou hadst been.
    Thus by degrees thy cause superior grew,
And the great end appeared at last in view:
We heard the people in thy hopes rejoice;
We saw the senate bending to thy voice;
The friends of Freedom hail'd the approaching reign
Of laws for which our fathers bled in vain;
While venal Faction, struck with new dismay,
Shrunk at their frown, and self-abandon'd lay.
Wak'd in the shock, the public Genius rose,
Abash'd and keener from his long repose;
Sublime in ancient pride, he rais'd the spear
Which slaves and tyrants long were wont to fear:
The city felt his call: from man to man,
From street to street the glorious horror ran;
Each crowded haunt was stirr'd beneath his power,
And, murmuring, challeng'd the deciding hour.
    Lo! the deciding hour at last appears;
The hour of every freeman's hopes and fears!

Thou, Genius! guardian of the Roman name,
O ever prompt tyrannic rage to tame!
Instruct the mighty moments as they roll,
And guide each movement steady to the goal.
Ye Spirits, by whose providential art
Succeeding motives turn the changeful heart,
Keep, keep the best in view to Curio's mind,
And watch his fancy, and his passions bind!
Ye Shades immortal, who, by Freedom led,
Or in the field, or on the scaffold bled,
Bend from your radiant seats a joyful eye,
And view the crown of all your labours nigh.
See Freedom mounting her eternal throne!
The sword submitted, and the laws her own:
See! public Power, chastis'd, beneath her stands,
With eyes intent, and uncorrupted hands!
See private life by wisest arts reclaim'd!
See ardent youth to noblest manners fram'd!
See us acquire whate'er was sought by you,
If Curio, only Curio, will be true.
'Twas then—O shame! O trust how ill repaid!
O Latium, oft by faithless sons betray'd!—
'Twas then—what frenzy on thy reason stole?
What spells unsinew'd thy determin'd soul?
—Is this the man in Freedom's cause approv'd?
The man so great, so honour'd, so belov'd?
This patient slave by tinsel chains allur'd?
This wretched suitor for a boon abjur'd?

This Curio, hated and despised by all?
Who fell himself, to work his country's fall?
   O lost, alike to action and repose!
Unknown, unpitied in the worst of woes!
With all that conscious, undissembled pride,
Sold to the insults of a foe defy'd!
With all that habit of familiar fame,
Doom'd to exhaust the dregs of life in shame!
The sole sad refuge of thy baffled art,
To act a statesman's dull exploded part,
Renounce the praise no longer in thy power,
Display thy virtue, though without a dower,
Contemn the giddy crowd, the vulgar wind,
And shut thy eyes that others may be blind.
—Forgive me, Romans, that I bear to smile
When shameless mouths your majesty defile,
Paint you a thoughtless, frantic, headlong crew,
And cast their own impieties on you.
For witness, Freedom, to whose sacred power
My soul was vow'd from reason's earliest hour,
How have I stood exulting, to survey
My country's virtues opening in thy ray!
How, with the sons of every foreign shore
The more I matched them, honour'd her's the more!
O race erect! whose native strength of soul,
—Which kings, nor priests, nor sordid laws control,
Bursts the tame round of animal affairs,
And seeks a nobler centre for its cares;

Intent the laws of life to comprehend,
And fix dominion's limits by its end.
Who, bold and equal in their love or hate,
By conscious reason judging every state,
The man forget not, though in rags he lies,
And know the mortal through a crown's disguise:
Thence prompt alike with witty scorn to view
Fastidious Grandeur lift his solemn brow,
Or, all awake at Pity's soft command,
Bend the mild ear, and stretch the gracious hand:
Thence large of heart, from envy far remov'd,
When public toils to virtue stand approv'd,
Not the young lover fonder to admire,
Nor more indulgent the delighted sire;
Yet high and jealous of their free-born name,
Fierce as the flight of Jove's destroying flame,
Where'er Oppression works her wanton sway,
Proud to confront, and dreadful to repay.
But if, to purchase Curio's sage applause,
My country must with him renounce her cause,
Quit with a slave the path a patriot trod,
Bow the meek knee, and kiss the regal rod;
Then still, ye powers, instruct his tongue to rail,
Nor let his zeal, nor let his subject fail:
Else, ere he change the style, bear me away
To where the Gracchi, where the Bruti stay!
    O long rever'd, and late resign'd to shame!
If this uncourtly page thy notice claim

When the loud cares of business are withdrawn
Nor well-drest beggars round thy footsteps fawn ;
In that still, thoughtful, solitary hour
When Truth exerts her unresisted power,
Breaks the false optics ting'd with Fortune's glare,
Unlocks the breast, and lays the passions bare ;
Then turn thy eyes on that important scene,
And ask thyself—if all be well within.
Where is the heartfelt worth and weight of soul,
Which labour could not stop, nor fear control ?
Where the known dignity, the stamp of awe,
Which half abash'd, the proud and venal saw ?
Where the calm triumphs of an honest cause ?
Where the delightful taste of just applause ?
Where the strong reason, the commanding tongue,
On which the senate fir'd or trembling hung ?
All vanish'd, all are sold—and in their room,
Couch'd in thy bosom's deep, distracted gloom,
See the pale form of barbarous Grandeur dwell,
Like some grim idol in a sorcerer's cell !
To her in chains thy dignity was led ;
At her polluted shrine thy honour bled ;
With blasted weeds thy awful brow she crown'd,
Thy powerful tongue with poison'd philters bound,
That baffled Reason straight indignant flew,
And fair Persuasion from her seat withdrew.
For now no longer Truth supports thy cause ;
No longer Glory prompts thee to applause ;

No longer Virtue breathing in thy breast,
With all her conscious majesty confest,
Still bright and brighter wakes the almighty flame,
To rouse the feeble, and the wilful tame,
And where she sees the catching glimpses roll,
Spreads the strong blaze, and all involves the soul;
But cold restraints thy conscious fancy chill,
And formal passions mock thy struggling will;
Or, if thy Genius e'er forget his chain,
And reach impatient at a nobler strain,
Soon the sad bodings of contemptuous mirth
Shoot through thy breast, and stab the generous birth,
Till, blind with smart, from Truth to Frenzy tost,
And all the tenour of thy reason lost,
Perhaps thy anguish drains a real tear;
While some with pity, some with laughter hear.
—Can Art, alas! or Genius, guide the head,
Where Truth and Freedom from the heart are fled?
Can lesser wheels repeat their native stroke,
When the prime function of the soul is broke?
　　But come, unhappy man! thy fates impend;
Come, quit thy friends, if yet thou hast a friend;
Turn from the poor rewards of guilt like thine,
Renounce thy titles, and thy robes resign;
For see the hand of Destiny display'd
To shut thee from the joys thou hast betray'd!
See the dire fane of Infamy arise!
Dark as the grave and spacious as the skies;

Where, from the first of time, thy kindred train,
The chiefs and princes of the unjust remain.
Eternal barriers guard the pathless road
To warn the wanderer of the curst abode ;
But prone as whirlwinds scour the passive sky,
The heights surmounted, down the steep they fly.
There, black with frowns, relentless Time awaits,
And goads their footsteps to the guilty gates :
And still he asks them of their unknown aims,
Evolves their secrets, and their guilt proclaims ;
And still his hands despoil them on the road
Of each vain wreath, by lying bards bestow'd,
Break their proud marbles, crush their festal cars,
And rend the lawless trophies of their wars.
At last the gates his potent voice obey ;
Fierce to their dark abode he drives his prey,
Where, ever arm'd with adamantine chains,
The watchful demon o'er her vassals reigns,
O'er mighty names and giant-powers of lust,
The Great, the Sage, the Happy, and August.
No gleam of hope their baleful mansion cheers,
No sound of honour hails their unblest ears ;
But dire reproaches from the friend betray'd,
The childless sire and violated maid ;
But vengeful vows for guardian laws effac'd
From towns enslav'd and continents laid waste ;
But long, Posterity's united groan,
And the sad charge of horrors not their own,

For ever through the trembling space resound,
And sink each impious forehead to the ground.
　Ye mighty foes of Liberty and Rest,
Give way, do homage to a mightier guest !
Ye daring spirits of the Roman race,
See Curio's toil your proudest claims efface !
—Aw'd at the name, fierce Appius rising bends,
And hardy Cinna from his throne attends :
'He comes,' they cry, 'to whom the Fates assign'd,
With surer arts to work what we design'd,
From year to year the stubborn herd to sway,
Mouth all their wrongs, and all their rage obey ;
Till, own'd their guide, and trusted with their power,
He mock'd their hopes in one decisive hour :
Then tir'd and yielding, led them to the chain,
And quenched the spirit we provoked in vain.'
　But thou, Supreme, by whose eternal hands
Fair Liberty's heroic empire stands ;
Whose thunders the rebellious deep control,
And quell the triumphs of the traitor's soul,
O turn this dreadful omen far away :
On Freedom's foes their own attempts repay ;
Relume her sacred fire so near supprest,
And fix her shrine in every Roman breast :
Though bold Corruption boast around the land,
'Let Virtue, if she can, my baits withstand !'
Though bolder now she urge the accursed claim,
Gay with her trophies rais'd on Curio's shame ;

G

Yet some there are who scorn her impious mirth,
Who know what conscience and a heart are worth.
—O friend and father of the human mind,
Whose art for noblest ends our frame designed!
If I, though fated to the studious shade
Which party-strife nor anxious power invade,
If I aspire in Public Virtue's cause,
To guide the Muses by sublimer laws,
Do thou her own authority impart,
And give my numbers entrance to the heart.
Perhaps the verse might rouse her smother'd flame,
And snatch the fainting patriot back to fame;
Perhaps, by worthy thoughts of human kind,
To worthy deeds exalt the conscious mind;
Or dash Corruption in her proud career,
And teach her slaves that Vice was born to fear.

CHARLES CHURCHILL

(Churchill's fame has steadily and deservedly sunk ever since his death, till almost the only interest left in him is on the one side historic, and on the other formal, this latter arising from the fact that he avowedly and successfully deserted Pope as a model, resorted to Dryden, and in doing this influenced Cowper, and, through Cowper, all the New School. A man of absolutely no morals, in any sense of the word, his constant affectations of moral indignation are half disgusting and half absurd. But his age thought him a very great political satirist, and he was actually one of no little power.)

THE CONFERENCE

GRACE said in form, which sceptics must agree,
When they are told that grace was said by me;
The servants gone, to break the scurvy jest
On the proud landlord, and his thread-bare guest;

The 'King' gone round, my lady too withdrawn,
My lord in usual taste began to yawn,
And lolling backward in his elbow-chair,
With an insipid kind of stupid stare,
Picking his teeth, twirling his seals about—
'Churchill, you have a poem coming out.
You've my best wishes; but I really fear
Your Muse in general is too severe;
Her spirit seems her int'rest to oppose,
And where she makes one friend, makes twenty foes.'
   C. Your lordship's fears are just, I feel their
      force,
But only feel it as a thing of course.
The man whose hardy spirit shall engage
To lash the vices of a guilty age,
At his first setting forward ought to know,
That ev'ry tongue he meets must be his foe;
That the rude breath of Satire will provoke
Many who feel, and more who fear the stroke.
But shall the partial rage of selfish men
From stubborn Justice wrench the righteous pen,
Or shall I not my settled course pursue,
Because my foes are foes to Virtue too?
   L. What is this boasted Virtue, taught in Schools,
And idly drawn from antiquated rules?
What is her use? Point out one wholesome end:
Will she hurt foes, or can she make a friend?
When from long fasts fierce appetites arise,

Can this same Virtue stifle Nature's cries?
Can she the pittance of a meal afford,
Or bid thee welcome to one great man's board?
When northern winds the rough December arm
With frost and snow, can Virtue keep thee warm?
Can'st thou dismiss the hard unfeeling dun
Barely by saying, thou art Virtue's son?
Or by base blund'ring statesmen sent to jail,
Will Mansfield take this Virtue for thy bail?
Believe it not, the name is in disgrace,
Virtue and Temple now are out of place.

   Quit then this meteor, whose delusive ray
From wealth and honour leads thee far astray.
True Virtue means, let Reason use her eyes,
Nothing with fools and int'rest with the wise.
Would'st thou be great, her patronage disclaim,
Nor madly triumph in so mean a name :
Let nobler wreaths thy happy brows adorn,
And leave to Virtue poverty and scorn.
Let Prudence be thy guide ; who doth not know
How seldom Prudence can with Virtue go?
To be successful try thy utmost force,
And Virtue follows as a thing of course.

   Hirco, who knows not Hirco? stains the bed
Of that kind master who first gave him bread,
Scatters the seeds of discord through the land,
Breaks ev'ry public, ev'ry private band,
Beholds with joy a trusting friend undone,

Betrays a brother, and would cheat a son :
What mortal in his senses can endure
The name of Hirco, for the wretch is poor !
'Let him hang, drown, starve, on a dunghill rot,
By all detested live, and die forgot ;
Let him, a poor return, in ev'ry breath
Feel all Death's pains, yet be whole years in death,'
Is now the gen'ral cry we all pursue :
Let Fortune change, and Prudence changes too ;
Supple and pliant a new system feels,
Throws up her cap, and spaniels at her heels ;
'Long live great Hirco,' cries, by int'rest taught,
'And let his foes, though I prove one, be naught.'
   C. Peace to such men, if such men can have
       peace,
Let their possessions, let their state increase ;
Let their base services in courts strike root,
And in the season bring forth golden fruit ;
I envy not : let those who have the will,
And with so little spirit, so much skill,
With such vile instruments their fortunes carve ;
Rogues may grow fat, an honest man dares starve.
   L. These stale conceits thrown off, let us advance
For once to real life, and quit romance.
Starve ! pretty talking ! but I fain would view
That man, that honest man, would do it too.
Hence to yon mountain which outbraves the sky,
And dart from pole to pole thy strengthen'd eye,

Through all that space you shall not view one man,
Not one, who dares to act on such a plan.
Cowards in calms will say, what in a storm
The brave will tremble at, and not perform.
Thine be the proof, and, spite of all you've said,
You'd give your honour for a crust of bread.
    C. What proof might do, what hunger might
        effect,
What famish'd Nature, looking with neglect
On all she once held dear, what fear, at strife
With fainting Virtue for the means of life,
Might make this coward flesh, in love with breath,
Shudd'ring at pain, and shrinking back from death,
In treason to my soul, descend to bear,
Trusting to Fate, I neither know nor care.
    Once, at this hour whose wounds afresh I feel,
Which nor prosperity nor time can heal,
Those wounds, which Fate severely hath decreed,
Mention'd or thought of, must for ever bleed,
Those wounds, which humbled all that pride of man,
Which brings such mighty aid to Virtue's plan;
Once, aw'd by Fortune's most oppressive frown,
By legal rapine to the earth bow'd down,
My credit at last gasp, my state undone,
Trembling to meet the shock I could not shun,
Virtue gave ground, and black despair prevail'd;
Sinking beneath the storm, my spirits fail'd,
Like Peter's faith; till one, a friend indeed,

May all distress find such in time of need !
One kind good man, in act, in word, in thought,
By Virtue guided, and by Wisdom taught,
Image of him whom Christians should adore,
Stretch'd forth his hand, and brought me safe to
    shore.
Since, by good fortune into notice rais'd,
And for some little merit largely prais'd,
Indulg'd in swerving from prudential rules,
Hated by rogues, and not belov'd by fools,
Plac'd above want, shall abject thirst of wealth
So fiercely war 'gainst my soul's dearest health,
That, as a boon, I should base shackles crave,
And, born to freedom, make myself a slave ;
That I should in the train of those appear,
Whom Honour cannot love, nor Manhood fear ?
    That I no longer skulk from street to street,
Afraid lest duns assail, and bailiff's meet ;
That I from place to place this carcase bear,
Walk forth at large, and wander free as air ;
That I no longer dread the awkward friend,
Whose very obligations must offend,
Nor, all too forward, with impatience burn,
At suff'ring favours which I can't return ;
That, from dependence and from pride secure,
I am not plac'd so high to scorn the poor,
Nor yet so low, that I my lord should fear,
Or hesitate to give him sneer for sneer ;

That, kind to others, to myself most true,
Feeling no want, I comfort those who do,
And with the will have power to aid distress :
These, and what other blessings I possess,
From the indulgence of the public rise ;
All private patronage my soul defies.
By candour more inclin'd to save, than damn,
A gen'rous Public made me what I am.
All that I have, they gave ; just Mem'ry bears
The grateful stamp, and what I am is theirs.

   L. To feign a red-hot zeal for Freedom's cause,
To mouth aloud for liberties and laws,
For public good to bellow all abroad,
Serves well the purposes of private fraud.
Prudence by public good intends her own ;
If you mean otherwise, you stand alone.
What do we mean by country and by court ?
What is it to oppose, what to support ?
Mere words of course, and what is more absurd
Than to pay homage to an empty word ?
Majors and minors differ but in name ;
Patriots and ministers are much the same ;
The only difference, after all their rout,
Is, that the one is *in*, the other *out*.

   Explore the dark recesses of the mind,
In the soul's honest volume read mankind,
And own, in wise and simple, great and small,
The same grand leading principle in all.

Whate'er we talk of wisdom to the wise,
Of goodness to the good, of public ties
Which to our country link, of private bands
Which claim most dear attention at our hands,
For parent and for child, for wife and friend,
Our first great mover, and our last great end,
Is one, and, by whatever name we call
The ruling tyrant, Self, is all in all.
This, which unwilling Faction shall admit,
Guided in diff'rent ways a Bute and Pitt,
Made tyrants break, made kings observe the law,
And gave the world a Stuart and Nassau.
    Hath Nature (strange and wild conceit of pride)
Distinguish'd thee from all her sons beside?
Doth Virtue in thy bosom brighter glow,
Or from a spring more pure doth action flow?
Is not thy soul bound with those very chains
Which shackle us ; or is that Self, which reigns
O'er kings and beggars, which in all we see
Most strong and sov'reign, only weak in thee?
Fond man, believe it not, experience tells
'Tis not thy virtue, but thy pride rebels.
Think (and for once lay by thy lawless pen)
Think, and confess thyself like other men ;
Think but one hour, and, to thy conscience led
By Reason's hand, bow down and hang thy head ;
Think on thy private life, recal thy youth,
View thyself now, and own with strictest truth,

That Self hath drawn thee from fair Virtue's way
Further than Folly would have dar'd to stray,
And that the talents lib'ral Nature gave
To make thee free, have made thee more a slave.
    Quit then, in prudence quit, that idle train
Of toys, which have so long abus'd thy brain,
And captive led thy pow'rs ; with boundless will
Let Self maintain her state and empire still,
But let her, with more worthy objects caught,
Strain all the faculties and force of thought
To things of higher daring ; let her range
Through better pastures, and learn how to change ;
Let her, no longer to weak Faction tied,
Wisely revolt, and join our stronger side.
    C. Ah ! what, my lord, hath private life to do
With things of public nature ?   Why to view
Would you thus cruelly those scenes unfold,
Which, without pain and horror to behold,
Must speak me something more or less than man ;
Which friends may pardon, but I never can ?
Look back ! a thought which borders on despair,
Which human nature must, yet cannot bear.
'Tis not the babbling of a busy world,
Where praise and censure are at random hurl'd,
Which can the meanest of my thoughts control,
Or shake one settled purpose of my soul.
Free and at large might their wild curses roam,
If all, if all, alas ! were well at home,

No—— 'tis the tale which angry Conscience tells,
When she with more than tragic horror swells
Each circumstance of guilt ; when stern, but true,
She brings bad actions forth into review ;
And, like the dread hand-writing on the wall,
Bids late Remorse awake at Reason's call ;
Arm'd at all points bids scorpion Vengeance pass,
And to the mind holds up Reflection's glass ;
The mind, which, starting, heaves the heartfelt groan,
And hates that form she knows to be her own.
   Enough of this—let private sorrows rest—
As to the public I dare stand the test ;
Dare proudly boast, I feel no wish above
The good of England, and my country's love.
Stranger to party-rage, by Reason's voice,
Unerring guide, directed in my choice,
Not all the tyrant pow'rs of Earth combin'd,
No, nor of Hell, shall make me change my mind.
What ! herd with men my honest soul disdains,
Men who, with servile zeal, are forging chains
For Freedom's neck, and lend a helping hand,
To spread destruction o'er my native land.
What ! shall I not, e'en to my latest breath,
In the full face of danger and of death,
Exert that little strength which Nature gave,
And boldly stem, or perish in the wave ?
   L. When I look backward for some fifty years,
And see *protesting* patriots turn to peers ;

Hear men, most loose, for decency declaim,
And talk of character without a name;
See infidels assert the cause of God,
And meek divines wield Persecution's rod;
See men transform'd to brutes, and brutes to men,
See Whitehead take a place, Ralph change his pen,
I mock the zeal, and deem the men in sport,
Who rail at ministers, and curse a court.
Thee, haughty as thou art, and proud in rhyme,
Shall some preferment, offer'd at a time
When Virtue sleeps, some sacrifice to pride,
Or some fair victim, move to change thy side.
Thee shall these eyes behold, to health restor'd,
Using, as Prudence bids, bold Satire's sword,
Galling thy present friends, and praising those,
Whom now thy frenzy holds thy greatest foes.
   C. May I (can worse disgrace on manhood fall)
Be born a Whitehead, and baptiz'd a Paul;
May I (though to his service deeply tied
By sacred oaths, and now by will allied)
With false feign'd zeal an injur'd God defend,
And use his name for some base private end;
May I (that thought bids double horrors roll
O'er my sick spirits, and unmans my soul)
Ruin the virtue which I held most dear,
And still must hold; may I, through abject fear,
Betray my friend; may to succeeding times,
Engrav'd on plates of adamant, my crimes

Stand blazing forth, whilst mark'd with envious blot,
Each little act of virtue is forgot;
Of all those evils which, to stamp men curs'd,
Hell keeps in store for vengeance, may the worst
Light on my head, and in my day of woe,
To make the cup of bitterness o'erflow,
May I be scorn'd by ev'ry man of worth,
Wander, like Cain, a vagabond on Earth,
Bearing about a Hell in my own mind,
Or be to Scotland for my life confin'd,
If I am one among the many known,
Whom Shelburne fled, and Calcraft blush'd to own.
    L. Do you reflect what men you make your foes?
    C. I do, and that's the reason I oppose.
Friends I have made, whom Envy must commend,
But not one foe, whom I would wish a friend.
What if ten thousand Butes and Hollands bawl,
One Wilkes hath made a large amends for all.
    'Tis not the title, whether handed down
From age to age, or flowing from the Crown
In copious streams on recent men, who came
From stems unknown, and sires without a name;
'Tis not the *star*, which our great Edward gave
To mark the virtuous, and reward the brave,
Blazing without, whilst a base heart within
Is rotten to the core with filth and sin;
'Tis not the tinsel grandeur, taught to wait,
At Custom's call, to mark a fool of state

From fools of lesser note, that soul can awe
Whose pride is reason, whose defence is law.
 L. Suppose (a thing scarce possible in art,
Were it thy cue to play a common part ;)
Suppose thy writing's so well fenc'd in law,
That Norton cannot find, nor make a flaw,
Hast thou not heard, that 'mongst our ancient tribes,
By party warpt, or lull'd asleep by bribes,
Or trembling at the ruffian hand of Force,
Law hath suspended stood, or chang'd its course ?
Art thou assur'd, that, for destruction ripe,
Thou may'st not smart beneath the self-same gripe ?
What sanction hast thou, frantic in thy rhymes,
Thy life, thy freedom to secure ?   .   .   .
                                        C. The times.
'Tis not on law, a system great and good,
By wisdom penn'd, and bought by noblest blood,
My faith relies : by wicked men and vain,
Law, once abus'd, may be abus'd again.
No, on our great Law-giver I depend,
Who knows and guides her to her proper end ;
Whose royalty of nature blazes out
So fierce, 'twere sin to entertain a doubt—
Did tyrant Stuarts now the laws dispense,
(Blest be the hour and hand which sent them hence)
For something, or for nothing, for a word,
Or thought, I might be doomed to death, *unheard*,
Life we might all resign to lawless pow'r,

Nor think it worth the purchase of an hour;
But Envy ne'er shall fix so foul a stain
On the fair annals of a Brunswick's reign.
　　If, slave to party, to revenge, or pride,
If, by frail human error drawn aside,
I break the law, strict rigour let her wear;
'Tis her's to punish, and 'tis mine to bear;
Nor by the voice of Justice doom'd to death,
Would I ask mercy with my latest breath.
But, anxious only for my country's good,
In which my king's, *of course*, is understood;
Form'd on a plan with some few patriot friends,
Whilst by just means I aim at noblest ends,
My spirits cannot sink; though from the tomb
Stern Jeffries should be placed in Mansfield's room;
Though he should bring, his base designs to aid,
Some *black attorney*, for his purpose made,
And shove, whilst Decency and Law retreat,
The modest Norton from his maiden seat;
Though both, in all confed'rates, should agree,
In damned league, to torture law and me,
Whilst George is king, I cannot fear endure;
Not to be guilty, is to be secure.
　　But when, in after-times, (be far remov'd
That day) our monarch, glorious and belov'd,
Sleeps with his fathers, should imperious Fate,
In vengeance, with fresh Stuarts curse our state;
Should they, o'erleaping ev'ry fence of law,

Butcher the brave to keep tame fools in awe ;
Should they, by brutal and oppressive force,
Divert sweet Justice from her even course ;
Should they, of ev'ry other means bereft,
Make my right hand a witness 'gainst my left ;
Should they, abroad by Inquisitions taught,
Search out my soul, and damn me for a thought ;
Still would I keep my course, still speak, still write,
Till Death had plung'd me in the shades of night.
　　Thou God of Truth, thou great, all-searching eye,
To whom our thoughts, our spirits open lie,
Grant me thy strength, and in that needful hour,
(Should it e'er come) when Law submits to Pow'r,
With firm resolve my steady bosom steel,
Bravely to suffer, though I deeply feel.
　　Let me, as hitherto, still draw my breath,
In love with life, but not in fear of death ;
And, if Oppression brings me to the grave,
And marks me dead, she ne'er shall mark a slave.
Let no unworthy marks of grief be heard,
No wild laments, not one unseemly word ;
Let sober triumphs wait upon my bier,
I won't forgive that friend who drops one tear.
Whether he's ravish'd in life's early morn,
Or, in old age, drops like an ear of corn,
Full ripe he falls, on Nature's noblest plan,
Who lives to Reason, and who dies a Man.

H

WILLIAM COWPER

*(Cowper's knowledge of politics was too much con-
ditioned by his secluded life and his terrible malady;
but the* Modern Patriot *is a gem.)*

THE MODERN PATRIOT

REBELLION is my theme all day,
   I only wish 'twould come
(As who knows but perhaps it may)
   A little nearer home.

Yon roaring boys who rave and fight
   On the other side the Atlantic,
I always held them in the right,
   But most so, when most frantic.

When lawless mobs insult the court,
   That man shall be my toast,
If breaking windows be the sport,
   Who bravely breaks the most.

The Modern Patriot

But oh ! for him my fancy culls
    The choicest flowers she bears,
Who constitutionally pulls
    Your house about your ears.

Such civil broils are my delight,
    Though some folks can't endure 'em,
Who say the mob are mad outright,
    And that a rope must cure 'em.

A rope !   I wish we patriots had
    Such strings for all who need 'em,—
What ! hang a man for going mad ?
    Then farewell British freedom.

'THE ROLLIAD'

(*The exceedingly amusing collection of anti-Pittite lampoons called* The Rolliad, Political Eclogues, Probationary Odes, *and so on, concocted chiefly by members of Brooks's club—may shock serious politicians by its purely personal and partisan character.* There is not a sentiment in it higher than the wish to get Smith out and Jones in, and, for that purpose, to make the most of the follies, blunders, and faults of Smith and Smith's friends. *But it is very amusing—more amusing, no doubt, as a whole than in samples, but still amusing after a fashion, of which I hope the following samples will give some taste.*)

ECLOGUE ON MARGARET NICHOLSON

THE Session up: the India-Bench appeas'd,
The Lansdownes satisfied, the Lowthers pleas'd,

Each job dispatch'd :—the Treasury boys depart,
As various fancy prompts each youthful heart,
Pitt, in chaste kisses seeking virtuous joy,
Begs Lady Chatham's blessing on her boy ;
While Mornington, as vicious as he can,
To fair R—l—n in vain affects the man :
With lordly Buckingham retir'd at Stowe,
Grenville, whose plodding brains no respite know,
To prove next year, how our finances thrive,
Schemes new reports, that two and two make five.
To plan of Eastern justice hies Dundas ;
And comely Villars to his votive glass ;
To embryo tax-bills Rose ; to dalliance Steele ;
And hungry hirelings to their hard-earn'd meal.
   A faithful pair, in mutual friendship tied,
Once keen in hate, as now in love allied,
(This, o'er admiring mobs in triumph rode,
Libell'd his Monarch, and blasphem'd his God ;
That, the mean drudge of tyranny and Bute,
At once his practis'd pimp and prostitute)
Adscomb's proud roof receives, whose dark recess
And empty vaults, its owner's mind express,
While block'd-up windows to the world display
How much he loves a tax, how much invites the day.
   Here the dire chance that god-like George befel,
How sick in spirit, yet in health how well ;
What Mayors by dozens, at the tale affrighted,
Got drunk, address'd, got laugh'd at, and got knighted ;

They read, with mingled horror and surprise,
In London's pure Gazette, that never lies.
Ye Tory bands, who taught by conscious fears,
Have wisely check'd your tongues, and sav'd your
      ears,—
Hear, ere hard fate forbids—what heav'nly strains
Flowed from the lips of these melodious swains.
Alternate was the song ; but first began,
With hands uplifted, the regenerate man.

WILKES

Bless'd be the beef-fed guard, whose rigorous twist
Wrench'd the rais'd weapon from the murderer's fist,
Him Lords in waiting shall with awe behold
In red tremendous, and hirsute in gold.
    On him, great monarch, let thy bounty shine,
What meed can match a life so dear as thine?
Well was that bounty measur'd, all must own,
That gave him *half* of what he sav'd—*a crown.*
    Bless'd the dull edge, for treason's views unfit,
Harmless as Sydney's rage, or Bearcroft's wit.
Blush clumsy patriots, for degenerate zeal,
Wilkes had not guided thus the faithless steel !
    Round your sad mistress flock, ye maids elect,
Whose charms severe your chastity protect ;
Scar'd by whose glance, despairing love descries,
That virtue steals no triumph from your eyes.

Round your bold master flock, ye mitred hive,
With anathems on Whigs his soul revive !
Saints ! whom the sight of human blood appals,
Save when to please the Royal will it falls.
   He breathes ! he lives ! the vestal choir advance,
Each takes a Bishop, and leads up the dance,
Nor dreads to break her long-respected vow,
For chaste—ah strange to tell !—are bishops now :
Saturnian times return !—the age of truth,
And—long foretold—is come, the virgin youth.
Now sage professors, for their learning's curse,
Die of their duty in remorseless verse :
Now sentimental Aldermen expire
In prose, half flaming with the Muses' fire ;
Theirs—while rich dainties swim on every plate,
Theirs the glad toil to feast for Britain's fate ;
Nor mean the gift the Royal grace affords,
—All shall be knights—but those that shall be lords.
   Fountain of Honour, that art never dry,
Touch'd with those drops of grace no thief can die,
Still with new titles soak the delug'd land,
Still may we all be safe from Ketch's menac'd hand !

JENKINSON

Oh wondrous man, with a more wond'rous Muse !
O'er my lank limbs thy strains a sleep diffuse,
Sweet as when Pitt with words disdaining end,

Toils to explain, yet scorns to comprehend.
Ah ! whither had we fled, had that foul day
Torn him untimely from our arms away ?
What ills had mark'd the age, had that dire thrust
Pierc'd his soft heart, and bow'd his bob to dust ?
Gods ! to my labouring sight what phantoms rise !
Here Juries triumph, and there droops Excise !
Fierce from defeat, and with collected might,
The low-born Commons claim the people's right :
And mad for freedom, vainly deem their own,
Their eye presumptuous dares to scan the throne.
See—in the general wreck that smothers all,
Just ripe for justice—see my Hastings fall :
Lo, the dear Major meets a rude repulse,
Though blazing in each hand he bears a *bulse* !
Nor Ministers attend, nor Kings relent,
Though rich Nabobs so splendidly repent.
See Eden's faith expos'd to sale again,
Who takes his plate, and learns his French in vain.
See countless eggs for us obscure the sky,
Each blanket trembles, and each pump is dry.
Far from good things Dundas is sent to roam,
Ah !—worse than banish'd—doom'd to live at home.
Hence dire illusions ! dismal scenes away—
Again he cries, ' What, what !' and all is gay.
    Come Brunswick, come, great king of loaves and
        fishes,
Be bounteous still to grant us all our wishes !

Twice every year with Beaufoy as we dine,
Pour'd to the brim—eternal George—be thine
Two foaming cups of his nectareous juice,
Which—new to gods,—no mortal vines produce.
To us shall Brudenell sing his choicest airs,
And capering Mulgrave ape the grace of bears;
A grand thanksgiving pious York compose,
In all the proud parade of pulpit prose;
For sure Omniscience will delight to hear,
Thou 'scapest a danger, that was never near.
While ductile Pitt thy whisper'd wish obeys,
While dupes believe whate'er the Doctor says,
While panting to be taxed, the famish'd poor
Grow to their chains, and only beg for more;
While fortunate in ill, thy servants find
No snares too slight to catch the vulgar mind:
Fix'd as the doom, thy pow'r shall still remain,
And thou, wise King, as uncontrol'd shalt reign.

WILKES

Thanks, *Jenky*, thanks, for ever could'st thou sing,
For ever could I sit, and hear thee praise the King.
Then take this book, which with a Patriot's pride,
Once to his sacred warrant I deny'd,
Fond though he was of reading all I wrote:
No gift can better suit thy tuneful throat.

JENKINSON

And thou this Scottish pipe, which Jamie's breath,
Inspir'd when living, and bequeath'd in death,
From lips unhallow'd I've preserv'd it long :
Take the just tribute of thy loyal song.

ODE   ·

BY MAJOR JOHN SCOTT, M.P.

I

WHY does the loitering sun retard his wain,
 When this glad hour demands a fiercer ray ?
Not so he pours his fire on Delhi's plain,
 To hail the Lord of Asia's natal day.
 There in mute pomp and cross-legg'd state,
 The *Raja Ponts* Mahommed Shah await.
   There *Malabar*,
   There *Bisnagar*,
There *Oude* and proud *Bahar*, in joy confederate.

II

Curs'd be the clime, and curs'd the laws, that lay
Insulting bonds on George's sovereign sway !

Arise, my soul, on wings of fire,
 To God's anointed, tune the lyre ;
Hail ! George, thou all-accomplish'd King !
 Just type of him who rules on high !
Hail ! inexhausted, boundless spring
 Of sacred truth and Holy Majesty !
Grand is thy form,—'bout five feet ten,
Thou well-built, worthiest, best of men !
Thy chest is stout, thy back is broad,—
Thy Pages view thee, and are aw'd !
Lo ! how thy white eyes roll !
Thy whiter eye-brows stare !
   Honest soul !
Thou'rt witty, as thou'rt fair.

III

North of the Drawing-room a closet stands :
The sacred nook, St. James's Park commands !
Here, in sequester'd state, great George receives
Memorials, treaties, and long lists of thieves !
Here all the force of sovereign thought is bent,
To fix Reviews, or change a government !
Heav'ns how each word with joy *Caermarthen* takes !
Gods ! how the lengthen'd chin of *Sydney* shakes !
 Blessing and bless'd the sage associate see,
 The proud triumphant league of incapacity.
  With subtile smiles,
  With innate wiles,

How do thy tricks of state, great George, abound.
    So in thy Hampton's mazy ground,
        The path that wanders
           In meanders,
           Ever bending,
           Never ending,
     Winding runs the eternal round
Perplex'd, involv'd, each thought bewilder'd moves ;
In short, quick turns the gay confusion roves ;
Contending themes the embarrass'd listener baulk,
Lost in the labyrinths of the devious talk !

            IV

Now shall the levee's ease thy soul unbend,
    Fatigu'd with Royalty's severer care !
Oh ! happy few ! whom brighter stars befriend,
    Who catch the chat—the witty whisper share !
          Methinks I hear
          In accents clear
Great Brunswick's voice still vibrate on my ear—
        ' What ?—what ?—what ?
        Scott !—Scott !—Scott !
        Hot !—hot !—hot !
        What ?—what ?—what ?'
     Oh ! fancy quick ! oh ! judgment true !
      Oh ! sacred oracle of regal taste !
    So hasty, and so generous too !

Not one of all thy questions will an answer wait!
Vain, vain, oh Muse, thy feeble art,
To paint the beauties of that head and heart!
That heart where all the virtues join!
That head that hangs on many a sign!

v

Monarch of mighty *Albion*, check thy talk!
Behold the *Squad* approach, led on by *Palk*!
Smith, Barwell, Call, Vansittart, form the band—
Lord of Britannia!—let them kiss thy hand!—
For *sniff*!—rich odours scent the sphere!
'Tis Mrs. Hastings' self brings up the rear!
God! how her diamonds flock
On each unpowdered lock!
On every membrane see a topaz clings!
Behold!—her joints are fewer than her rings!
Illustrious dame! on either ear,
The Munny Begums' spoils appear!
Oh! Pitt, with awe behold that precious throat,
Whose necklace teems with many a future vote!
Pregnant with *Burgage* gems each hand she rears;
And lo! depending questions gleam upon her ears!
Take her great George, and shake her by the hand;
'Twill loose her jewels and enrich thy land.
But oh! reserve one ring for an old stager;
The *ring* of future marriage for her *Major*!

RONDEAU

AROUND the tree, so fair, so green,
Erewhile, when summer shone serene,
    Lo, where the leaves in many a ring
    Before the wintry tempest wing,
Fly scattered o'er the dreary scene :

Such, NORTH, thy friends.   Now cold and keen
Thy Winter blows ; no sheltering screen
    They stretch, no graceful shade they fling
                     Around the tree.

Yet grant, just Fate, each wretch so mean,
Like Eden, pining in his spleen
    For posts, for stars, for strings, may swing
    On two stout posts in hempen string.
Few eyes would drop a tear, I ween,
                     Around the tree.

EPIGRAM

On *fair and equal* terms to place
    An union is thy care :
But trust me, Powis, in this case
The *equal* should not please his Grace
    And Pitt dislikes the *fair*.

PETER PINDAR

(*Two almost insurmountable difficulties lie before the selector from Wolcot—his fluent inequality, which constantly merges capital lines or stanzas in oceans not exactly of dulness but of matter scarcely remarkable, and his extreme dirtiness. He is, I should think, for the same reasons, very little read nowadays; but if these selections send any one to him, the person sent, will I think be rewarded, and I, the sender, shall not blush.*)

APPLE DUMPLINGS

'AN APOLOGETIC POSTSCRIPT TO *ODE UPON ODE*'

ONCE on a time, a monarch, tir'd with whooping,
    Whipping and spurring,
    Happy in worrying
  A poor, defenceless, harmless buck
  (The horse and rider wet as muck),
From his high consequence and wisdom stooping,

Enter'd, through curiosity, a cot,
Where sat a poor old woman and her pot.

The wrinkled, blear-ey'd, good, old granny,
In this same cot, illum'd by many a cranny,
  Had finish'd apple dumplings for her pot :
In tempting row the naked dumplings lay,
When, lo ! the monarch, in his usual way,
Like lightning spoke, 'What's this ? what's this ?
        what ? what ? '

Then taking up a dumpling in his hand,
His eyes with admiration did expand—
  And oft did majesty the dumpling grapple :
' 'Tis monstrous, monstrous hard, indeed,' he cry'd :
What makes it, pray, so hard ? '—The dame reply'd,
  Low curt'sying, ' Please your majesty, the apple.'

' Very astonishing, indeed !—strange thing ! '
(Turning the dumpling round, rejoin'd the king),
    ' 'Tis most extraordinary then, all this is—
    It beats Pinetti's conjuring all to pieces—
Strange I should never of a dumpling dream—
But, goody, tell me where, where, where's the seam ? '

' Sir, there's no seam,' quoth she ; ' I never knew
That folks did apple dumplings *sew*.'—

I

'No!' cry'd the staring monarch with a grin,
'How, how the devil got the apple in?'

On which the dame the curious scheme reveal'd
By which the apple lay so sly conceal'd,
    Which made the Solomon of Britain start;
Who to the Palace with full speed repair'd,   ·
And queen and princesses so beauteous scar'd,
    All with the wonders of the dumpling art!

There did he labour one whole week, to show
    The wisdom of an *apple-dumpling maker*;
And, lo! so deep was majesty in dough,
    The palace seem'd the lodging of a *baker*.

INSTRUCTIONS TO A CELEBRATED LAUREAT, *alias* THE PROGRESS OF CURIOSITY, *alias* A BIRTH-DAY ODE, *alias* MR. WHITBREAD'S BREWHOUSE

    *   *   *   *   *

Now majesty, alive to knowledge, took
A very pretty memorandum-book,
With gilded leaves of asses' skin so white,
And in it legibly began to write—

Memorandum

A charming place beneath the grates,
For roasting chesnuts or potates.

Mem.

'Tis hops that give a bitterness to beer——
Hops grow in Kent, says Whitbread, and elsewhere.

Quære

Is there no cheaper stuff? where doth it dwell?
Would not horse-aloes bitter it as well?

Mem.

To try it soon on our small beer—
'Twill save us sev'ral pounds a year.—

Mem.—To remember to forget to ask
Old Whitbread to my house one day—

Mem.

Not to forget to take of beer the cask,
The brewer offer'd me, away.

Now having pencil'd his remarks so shrewd ;
　Sharp as the point, indeed, of a new pin ;
His majesty his watch most sagely view'd,
　And then put up his asses' skin.

To Whitbread now deign'd majesty to say,
'Whitbread, are all your horses fond of hay ?'
'Yes, please your majesty,' in humble notes,
The brewer answer'd—'also, sir, of oats :
Another thing my horses too maintains—
And that, an't please your majesty, are grains.'

'Grains, grains,' said majesty, 'to fill their crops ?
Grains, grains—that comes from hops—yes, hops,
　　hops, hops.'
Here was the king, like hounds sometimes at fault—
　'Sire,' cry'd the humble brewer, 'give me leave
　Your sacred majesty to undeceive :
Grains, sire, are never made from hops, but malt.'

'True,' said the cautious monarch, with a smile :
From malt, malt, malt—I meant malt all the while.'
'Yes,' with the sweetest bow, rejoin'd the brewer,
'An't please your majesty, you did, I'm sure.'
'Yes,' answer'd majesty, with quick reply,
'I did, I did, I did, I, I, I, I.'

Now this was wise in Whitbread—here we find
A very pretty knowledge of mankind :
As monarchs never must be in the wrong,
'Twas really a bright thought in Whitbread's tongue,
To tell a little fib or some such thing,
To save the sinking credit of a king.

Some brewers, in the rage of information,
Proud to instruct the *ruler* of a nation,
Had on the folly *dwelt*, to seem damn'd clever !
Now, what had been the consequence ? Too plain !
The man had cut his consequence in twain ;
The king had hated the *wise* fool for ever !

LIBERTY'S LAST SQUEAK

FAREWEL, O my pen and my tongue !
   To part with such friends I am loath ;
But Pitt, in majorities strong,
   Voweth horrible vengeance on both.

No more on a king or a queen,
   Apple-dumpling, and smuggling so sweet ;
Like their stomachs your wit shall be keen,
   Hogs, hay, and fat bullocks, and wheat.

No more upon smugglers at court,
   Mother Schwellenberg, bulses, and shawls ;

Nor at levees and drawing-rooms sport,
 Where man the poor sycophant *crawls*.

The meanness no more of *high folk*
 In the rope of your satire shall swing :
For, behold, there is death in the joke
 That squinteth at queen or at king.

Thus untax'd by your satire, my friends,
 Courts smile at th' intended decree ;
Thus the reign of poor ridicule ends,
 And follies, like shawls, will *go free*.

Yes Folly will prattle and grin
 With her scourges Oppression will rise,
Since satire's a damnable sin,
 And a sin to be virtuous and wise.

But wherefore not laugh at a ——?
 And wherefore not laugh at a ——?
A laugh is a laudable thing,
 When people are silly and mean.

When we paid civil list without strife,
 When we paid the old quack for his cure,
When we pray'd at Peg Nicholson's knife,
 The k—— laughed at us, to be sure.

Ev'n the minions of courts will escape;
    Dundas, Pitt, and Jenky, and Rose,
Yes, Satire gets into a scrape,
    If she takes the four R——s by the nose.

No more must ye laugh at an ass;
    No more run on topers a rig,
Since Pitt gets as drunk as Dundas,
    And Dundas gets as drunk as a pig.

A laugh at a delegate hurts;
    Yes, 'twere dangerous to hazard your sneers;
And mock the sweet *mercy* of courts,
    That return'd him his forfeited ears.

Now farewel to fair Buckingham-house,
    To Windsor, and Richmond, and Kew;
Farewel to the tale of the L—— !
    Mother Red-cap, and Monarchs, adieu !

Like ferrets, since all must be muzzled,
    (And *muzzled* indeed we shall *be* !)
Say Pitt (for I'm grievously puzzled),
    May we venture a *horse-laugh* at thee ?'

SIXTH ODE TO INS AND OUTS

WHEN Pitt was out of office push'd,
   What horror smote the levee mob?
Mad into street of Downing rush'd
   His minions, always ready for a *job* :

   A most obsequious *stud* of hacks,
   Who bore him on their humble backs
Through *dirty lanes*, through thick and thin ;
   No matter what the object, no ;
   When Pitt *commands—it must be so* ;
Whether to *clothe* the naked realm, or *skin*.

   Muse, would it be too harsh to say,
   The tumult on that kick-out day
Was mob-like at a house on fire ;
   Where *friends*, amid the conflagration,
   With a kind thief-acceleration,
Whip off the goods they guarded by *desire* ?

   Unfeeling as a stone, or harder,
   In rush'd Lord G———— to the larder,
Caught up a goose for self and wife ;
   In ran Dundas with hungry paunch,
   Snatch'd up a turbot and a haunch :

In bounc'd Charles Long, and, with his butcher's
        knife,
   (For in the plunder *he* must also join),
   And cut off slices from a fat *sirloin*.

In scamper'd Windham—'Where's *my* share?
   I *must* be partner in the spoils':
Then up he caught an old jack hare,
   A *proper* present for his toils:

   '*I* must have something,' Canning cries,
   And fastens on some rich mince-pies,
As dext'rous as the rest to rifle:
   Ecod! and he must something do
   For *mother* and for *sisters* too,
So steals some syllabubs and *trifle*.

   But where was Justice all the while,
   That things were going off *in style?*
Poor gentlewoman! she was gagg'd and bound;
   Her even scales, alas! abhorr'd,
   In pieces broken with her sword;
Nor were the fasces to be found.

   Such were the *guardians* of the state,
Just like a shoal of sharks who swam in,
   With maws as wide as the park gate,
To save (by eating us) from *famine*!

A MORAL CONCLUSION

In this world's wild, uncertain chase,
What strange events at times take place !
Some bright with *joy*, some black with *sorrow* !
Omnium est rerum vicissitudo !
To-day what wonders *I* and *you* do,
That happen not again *to-morrow* !

Hawkesb'ry, and Windham, Canning, Long,
Were *under-strappers* to Will Pitt ;
Forerunners, oft they gave their tongue
Before the great man pour'd his wit.

Thus Paul's four small clock-quarters ('prentice
        boys)
Instruct their mighty master when to sound :
Paul solemn listens to the tinkling noise,
Then breaks in thunder to the world around !

But herald under-strappers now no more,
Pitt out of office, the broad farce is o'er ;
Flung from his pedestal amid the rabble,
Deep-thundering Pitt is—poor old Goody Gabble.

Ah me! *sic transit gloria mundi*—
Such things will *be* till moon and sun die,
And earth our ashes, our pale embers cover:
And really, when we sum up *all*,
What's life?—A blast—a little squall.—
Death's calm must come at last, and all *is over*—
All in our tombs in peace—not *one*
To read '*Hic jacet*' on the *stone*!

'THE ANTI-JACOBIN'

(I cannot help it if these immortal things are hackneyed; they must reappear.)

THE FRIEND OF HUMANITY
AND THE KNIFE-GRINDER

FRIEND OF HUMANITY

'NEEDY Knife-grinder! whither are you going?
Rough is the road, your wheel is out of order—
Bleak blows the blast;—your hat has got a hole in't,
   So have your breeches!

'Weary Knife-grinder! little think the proud ones,
Who in their coaches roll along the turnpike-
-road, what hard work 'tis crying all day "Knives and
   Scissors to grind O!"

'Tell me, Knife-grinder, how came you to grind
    knives?
Did some rich man tyrannically use you?
Was it the squire? or parson of the parish?
                            Or the attorney?

'Was it the squire, for killing of his game? or
Covetous parson, for his tithes distraining?
Or roguish lawyer, made you lose your little
                            All in a lawsuit?

'(Have you not read the Rights of Man, by Tom
    Paine?)
Drops of compassion tremble on my eyelids,
Ready to fall, as soon as you have told your
                            Pitiful story.'

KNIFE-GRINDER

'Story! God bless you! I have none to tell, sir,
Only last night a-drinking at the Chequers,
This poor old hat and breeches, as you see, were
                            Torn in a scuffle.

'Constables came up for to take me into
Custody; they took me before the justice;
Justice Oldmixon put me in the parish-
                            Stocks for a vagrant.

' I should be glad to drink your Honour's health in
A pot of beer, if you will give me sixpence;
But for my part, I never love to meddle
                    with politics, sir.'

FRIEND OF HUMANITY

' *I* give thee sixpence ! I will see thee damn'd first—
Wretch ! whom no sense of wrongs can rouse to ven-
        geance—
Sordid, unfeeling, reprobate, degraded,
                    Spiritless outcast ! '

[*Kicks the Knife-grinder, overturns his wheel, and exit
    in a transport of Republican enthusiasm and uni-
    versal philanthropy.*]

LA SAINTE GUILLOTINE

A NEW SONG, ATTEMPTED FROM THE FRENCH

Tune, ' O'er the vine-cover'd hills and gay regions of France.'

I

FROM the blood bedew'd valleys and mountains of
        France,
See the Genius of Gallic invasion advance !

Old ocean shall waft her, unruffled by storm,
While our shores are all lined with the *Friends of
    Reform.*
Confiscation and Murder attend in her train,
With meek-eyed Sedition, the daughter of Paine ;
While her sportive *Poissardes* with light footsteps are
    seen
To dance in a ring round the gay *Guillotine.*

II

To *London,* 'the rich, the defenceless,' she comes—
'Hark! my boys, to the sound of the Jacobin drums!
See Corruption, Prescription, and Privilege fly,
Pierced through by the glance of her blood-darting
    eye.
While patriots, from prison and prejudice freed,
In soft accents shall lisp the Republican Creed,
And with tricolour'd fillets, and cravats of green,
Shall crowd round the altar of *Sainte Guillotine.*'

III

See the level of Freedom sweeps over the land—
The vile Aristocracy's doom is at hand!
Not a seat shall be left in a House *that we know,*
But for *Earl Buonaparte* and *Baron Moreau.*—

But the rights of the Commons shall still be respected,
Buonaparte himself shall approve the elected
And the Speaker shall march with majestical mien,
And make his three bows to the grave *Guillotine.*

IV

Two heads, says the proverb, are better than one,
But the Jacobin choice is for Five Heads or none.
By Directories only can Liberty thrive;
Then down with the ONE, Boys! and up with the
    FIVE!
How our bishops and judges will stare with amaze-
    ment,
When their heads are thrust out at the *National Case-
ment*!
When the *National Razor* has shaved them quite
    clean,
What a handsome oblation to *Sainte Guillotine*!

THE SOLDIER'S FRIEND

DACTYLICS

COME, little Drummer Boy, lay down your knapsack
    here:
I am the Soldier's Friend—here are some books for
    you;
Nice clever books by Tom Paine, the philanthropist.

Here's half-a-crown for you—here are some handbills
　　too—
Go to the Barracks, and give all the Soldiers some.
Tell them the Sailors are all in a Mutiny.
　　[*Exit Drummer Boy, with Handbills and Half-
　　a-crown.—Manet Soldier's Friend.*

Liberty's friends thus all learn to amalgamate,
Freedom's volcanic explosion prepares itself,
Despots shall bow to the Fasces of Liberty,
　　Reason, philosophy, 'fiddledum diddledum,'
　　Peace and Fraternity, 'higgledy, piggledy,'
Higgledy, piggledy, 'fiddledum diddledum.'
　　　　　　　Et cætera, et cætera, et cætera.

ACME AND SEPTIMIUS;

OR,

THE HAPPY UNION

CELEBRATED AT THE CROWN AND ANCHOR TAVERN

　　Fox, with Tooke to grace his side,
　　Thus address'd his blooming bride—
　　'Sweet! should I e'er, in power or place,
　　Another Citizen embrace;

K

Should e'er my eyes delight to look
On ought alive, save John Horne Tooke,
Doom me to ridicule and ruin,
In the coarse hug of *Indian* Bruin!'

He spoke; and to the left and right,
N—rf—lk hiccupp'd with delight.

Tooke, his bald head gently moving,
    On the sweet Patriot's drunken eyes,
    His wine-empurpled lips applies,
And thus returns in accents loving:

'So, my dear Charley, may success
At length my ardent wishes bless,
And lead through Discord's low'ring storm,
To one grand RADICAL REFORM!
As from this hour I love thee more
Than e'er I hated thee before!'

He spoke, and to the left and right,
N—rf—lk hiccupp'd with delight.

With this good omen they proceed;
Fond toasts their mutual passion feed;
In Fox's breast Horne Tooke prevails
Before rich *Ireland* and *South Wales*;
And Fox (un-read each other book),

Is Law and Gospel to Horne Tooke.

When were such kindred souls united!
Or wedded pair so much delighted?

LINES

WRITTEN BY A TRAVELLER AT CZARCO-ZELO UNDER THE BUST OF A CERTAIN ORATOR, ONCE PLACED BETWEEN THOSE OF DEMOSTHENES AND CICERO.

I

THE Grecian Orator of old,
With scorn rejected Philip's laws,
Indignant spurn'd at foreign gold,
And triumph'd in his country's cause.

II

A foe to every wild extreme,
'Mid civil storms, the Roman Sage
Repress'd Ambition's frantic scheme,
And check'd the madding people's rage.

III

Their country's peace, and wealth, and fame,
With patriot zeal their labours sought,

And Rome's or Athens' honour'd name
Inspired and govern'd every thought.

IV

Who now in this presumptuous hour,
Aspires to share the Athenian's praise?
—The advocate of foreign power,
The Æschines of later days.

V

What chosen name to Tully's join'd,
Is thus announced to distant climes?
—Behold, to lasting shame consign'd,
The Catiline of modern times!

THE PROGRESS OF MAN

FIRST INSTALMENT

Whether some great, supreme o'er-ruling Power
Stretch'd forth its arm at nature's natal hour,
Composed this mighty whole with plastic skill,
Wielding the jarring elements at will?
Or whether sprung from Chaos' mingling storm,
The mass of matter started into form?

Or Chance o'er earth's green lap spontaneous fling
The fruits of autumn and the flowers of spring?
Whether material substance unrefined,
Owns the strong impulse of instinctive mind,
Which to one centre points diverging lines,
Confounds, refracts, invig'rates, and combines;
Whether the joys of earth, the hopes of heaven,
By Man to God, or God to Man were given?
If virtue leads to bliss, or vice to woe?
Who rules above, or who reside below?
Vain questions all—shall Man presume to know?
On all these points, and points obscure as these,
Think they who will,—and think whate'er they please!

Let us a plainer, steadier theme pursue—
Mark the grim savage scoop his light canoe;
Mark the dark rook on pendent branches hung,
With anxious fondness feed her cawing young.—
Mark the fell leopard through the desert prowl,
Fish prey on fish, and fowl regale on fowl;
How Lybian tigers' chawdrons love assails,
And warms, midst seas of ice, the melting whales;
Cools the crimpt cod, fierce pangs to perch imparts,
Shrinks shrivell'd shrimps, but opens oysters' hearts;—
Then say, how all these things together tend
To one great truth, prime object, and good end?
First—to each living thing, whate'er its kind,
Some lot, some part, some station is assign'd.

The feather'd race with pinions skim the *air*—
Not so the mackerel, and still less the bear :
This roams the *wood*, carniv'rous, for his prey ;
That with soft roe, pursues his *watery* way :—
This slain by hunters yields his shaggy hide ;
That, caught by fishers, is on *Sundays* cried.—

But each contented with his humble sphere,
Moves unambitious through the circling year ;
Nor e'er forgets the fortune of his race,
Nor pines to quit, or strives to change his place.
Ah ! who has seen the mailèd lobster rise,
Clap her broad wings, and soaring claim the skies ?
When did the owl, descending from her bow'r,
Crop, 'midst the fleecy flocks, the tender flow'r ;
Or the young heifer plunge, with pliant limb,
In the salt wave, and fish-like strive to swim ?

The same with plants—potatoes 'tatoes breed,—⎫
Uncostly cabbage springs from cabbage seed ;   ⎬
Lettuce to lettuce, leeks to leeks succeed ;   ⎭
Nor e'er did cooling cucumbers presume
To flow'r like myrtle, or like violets bloom.
—Man, only,—rash, refined presumptuous Man,
Starts from his rank, and mars creation's plan.
Born the free heir of nature's wide domain,
To art's strict limits bounds his narrow'd reign ;
Resigns his native rights for meaner things,
For Faith and Fetters—Laws, and Priests, and Kings.

THE PROGRESS OF MAN

THIRD INSTALMENT.—MARRIAGE

EXTRACT

HAIL ! beauteous lands that crown the Southern Seas ;
Dear happy seats of Liberty and Ease !
Hail ! whose green coasts the peaceful ocean laves,
Incessant washing with his watery waves !
Delicious islands ! to whose envied shore
Thee, gallant Cook ! the ship Endeavour bore.

There laughs the sky, there Zephyr's frolic train,
And light-wing'd loves, and blameless pleasures reign :
There, when two souls congenial ties unite,
No hireling *Bonzes* chant the mystic rite ;
Free every thought, each action unconfined,
And light those fetters which no rivets bind.

There in each grove, each sloping bank along,
And flow'rs and shrubs and odorous herbs among,
Each shepherd clasp'd, with undisguised delight,
His yielding fair one,—in the Captain's sight :
Each yielding fair, as chance or fancy led,
Preferr'd new lovers to her sylvan bed.

Learn hence, each nymph, whose free aspiring
    mind
Europe's cold laws, and colder customs bind—
O! learn, what Nature's genial laws decree—
What Otaheite is, let Britain be!

*   *   *   *   *   *   *

Of WHIST or CRIBBAGE mark the amusing game—
The Partners *changing*, but the SPORT the *same*.
Else would the Gamester's anxious ardour cool,
Dull every deal, and stagnant every pool.
—Yet must *one* Man, with one unceasing Wife,
Play the LONG RUBBER of connubial life.

Yes! human laws, and laws esteem'd divine,
The generous passion straiten and confine;
And, as a stream, when art constrains its course,
Pours its fierce torrent with augmented force,
So, Passion narrow'd to one channel small,
Unlike the former, does not flow at all.
—For Love *then* only flaps his purple wings,
When uncontroll'd by Priestcraft or by Kings.

Such the strict rules that, in these barbarous climes,
Choke youth's fair flow'rs, and feelings turn to crimes:
And people every walk of polish'd life,
With that two-headed monster, MAN and WIFE.

Yet bright examples sometimes we observe,
Which from the general practice seem to swerve;
Such as presented to Germania's view,
A Kotzbue's bold emphatic pencil drew;
Such as, translated in some future age,
Shall add new glories to the British stage;
—While the moved audience sit in dumb despair,
'Like Hottentots, *and at each other stare.*'

With look sedate, and staid beyond her years,
In matron weeds a *Housekeeper* appears.
The jingling keys her comely girdle deck—
Her 'kerchief colour'd, and her apron *check*.
Can that be Adelaide, that 'soul of whim,'
Reform'd in practice, and in manner prim?
—On household cares intent, with many a sigh
She turns the pancake, and she moulds the pie;
Melts into sauces rich the savoury ham
From the crush'd berry strains the lucid jam;
Bids brandied cherries, by infusion slow,
Imbibe new flavour, and their own forego,
Sole cordial of her heart, sole solace of her woe!
While still, responsive to each mournful moan,
The saucepan simmers in a softer tone.

     *   *   *   *   *   *   *

A CONSOLATORY ADDRESS
TO HIS GUN-BOATS

BY CITIZEN MUSKEIN

O navis referent in mare te novi fluctus.

O GENTLE GUN-BOATS, whom the Seine
Discharged from Havre to the main;
Now leaky, creaking, blood-bespatter'd,
With rudders broken, canvas shatter'd—
O tempt the treacherous sea no more,
But gallantly regain the shore.

   Scarce could our guardian Goddess, Reason,
Ensure your timbers through the season.
Though built of wood from famed Marseilles,
Well mann'd from galleys, and from jails,
Though with Lepaux's and Rewbell's aid,
By Pleville's skill your keel was laid;
Though lovely Stael, and lovelier Stone,
Have work'd their fingers to the bone,
And cut their petticoats to rags
To make your bright Three Colour'd Flags;
Yet sacrilegious grape and ball
Deform the works of Stone and Stael,
And trembling, without food or breeches,
Our sailors curse the *painted* ————.

Children of Muskein's anxious care,
Source of my hope and my despair,
GUN-BOATS—unless you mean hereafter—
To furnish food for British laughter—
Sweet GUN-BOATS, with your gallant crew,
Tempt not the rocks of SAINT MARCOU;
Beware the Badger's bloody pennant,
And that d——d invalid LIEUTENANT!

ELEGY ON THE DEATH
OF JEAN BON ST. ANDRÉ

I

ALL in the town of Tunis,
In Africa the torrid,
On a Frenchman of rank
Was play'd such a prank,
As Lepaux must think quite horrid.

II

No story half so shocking,
By kitchen fire or laundry,
Was ever heard tell,—
As that which befell
The great Jean Bon St. André.

III

Poor John was a gallant Captain,
In battles much delighting ;
  He fled full soon
  On the First of June—
But he bade the rest keep fighting.

IV

To Paris then returning,
And recover'd from his panic,
  He translated the plan
  Of Paine's Rights of Man,
Into language Mauritanic.

V

He went to teach at Tunis—
Where as Consul he was settled—
  Amongst other things,
  'That the people are kings !'
Whereat the Dey was nettled.

VI

The Moors being rather stupid,
And in temper somewhat mulish,
  Understood not a word
  Of the Doctrine they heard,
And thought the Consul foolish.

VII

He form'd a *Club* of *Brothers*,
And moved some resolutions—
  'Ho! Ho! (says the Dey),
  So this is the way
That the French make *Revolutions.*'

VIII

The Dey then gave his orders
In Arabic and Persian—
  'Let no more be said—
  But bring me his head!—
These *Clubs* are my aversion.'

IX

The Consul quoted Wicquefort,
And Puffendorf and Grotius:
  And proved from Vattel
  Exceedingly well,
Such a deed would be quite atrocious.

X

'Twould have moved a Christian's bowels
To hear the doubts he stated;
  But the Moors they did
  As they were bid,
And strangled him while he prated.

XI

His head with a sharp-edged sabre
They severed from his shoulders,
  And stuck it on high,
  Where it caught the eye,
To the wonder of all beholders.

XII

This sure is a doleful story
As e'er you heard or read of;—
  If at Tunis you prate
  Of matters of state,
Anon they cut your head off!

XIII

But we hear the French Directors
Have thought the point so knotty;
  That the Dey having shewn
  He dislikes Jean Bon,
They have sent him Bernadotte.

NEW MORALITY

FROM mental mists to purge a nation's eyes;
To animate the weak, unite the wise;
To trace the deep infection, that pervades
The crowded town, and taints the rural shades;
To mark how wide extends the mighty waste
O'er the fair realms of Science, Learning, Taste;
To drive and scatter all the brood of lies,
And chase the varying falsehood as it flies;
The long arrears of ridicule to pay,
To drag reluctant Dullness back to-day;
Much yet remains.—To you these themes belong,
Ye favour'd sons of virtue and of song!

Say, is the field too narrow? are the times
Barren of folly, and devoid of crimes?

Yet, venial vices, in a milder age,
Could rouse the warmth of Pope's satiric rage;
The doating miser, and the lavish heir,
The follies, and the foibles of the fair,
Sir Job, Sir Balaam, and old Euclio's thrift,
And Sappho's diamonds with her dirty shift,
Blunt, Charteris, Hopkins,—meaner subjects fired
The keen-eyed Poet; while the Muse inspired
Her ardent child,—entwining, as he sate,
His laurell'd chaplet with the thorns of hate.

But say,—indignant does the Muse retire,
Her shrine deserted, and extinct its fire?
No pious hand to feed the sacred flame,
No raptured soul a poet's charge to claim?

Bethink thee, G—ff—rd; when some future age
Shall trace the promise of thy playful page;—
'The hand which brush'd a swarm of fools away,
Should rouse to grasp a more reluctant prey!'—
Think then, will pleaded indolence excuse
The tame secession of thy languid Muse?

Ah! where is now thy promise? why so long
Sleep the keen shafts of satire and of song?
Oh! come with Taste and Virtue at thy side,
With ardent zeal inflamed, and patriot pride;
With keen poetic glance direct the blow,
And empty all thy quiver on the foe:
No pause—no rest—till weltering on the ground
The poisonous hydra lies, and pierced with many a
wound.

Thou too!—the nameless Bard,—whose honest
zeal
For law, for morals, for the public weal,
Pours down impetuous on thy country's foes
The stream of verse, and many-languaged prose;

Thou too !—though oft thy ill-advised dislike
The guiltless head with random censure strike,—
Though quaint allusions, vague and undefined,
Play faintly round the ear, but mock the mind;
Through the mix'd mass yet truth and learning shine
And manly vigour stamps the nervous line;
And patriot warmth the generous rage inspires,
And wakes and points the desultory fires !

Yet more remain unknown : for who can tell
What bashful genius, in some rural cell,
As year to year, and day succeeds to day,
In joyless leisure wastes his life away ?
In him the flame of early fancy shone ;
His genuine worth his old companions own ;
In childhood and in youth their chief confess'd,
His master's pride, his pattern to the rest.
Now far aloof retiring from the strife
Of busy talents, and of active life,
As, from the loopholes of retreat, he views
Our stage, verse, pamphlets, politics, and news,
He loaths the world,—or, with reflection sad,
Concludes it irrecoverably mad ;
Of taste, of learning, morals, all bereft,
No hope, no prospect to redeem it, left.

Awake ! for shame ! or e'er thy nobler sense
Sink in the oblivious pool of indolence !

L

Must wit be found alone on falsehood's side,
Unknown to truth, to virtue unallied?
Arise! nor scorn thy country's just alarms;
Wield in her cause thy long-neglected arms:
Of lofty satire pour the indignant strain,
Leagued with her friends, and ardent to maintain,
'Gainst Learning's, Virtue's, Truth's, Religion's foes,
A kingdom's safety, and the world's repose.

If Vice appal thee,—if thou view with awe
Insults that brave, and crimes that 'scape the law;—
Yet may the specious bastard brood, which claim
A spurious homage under Virtue's name,
Sprung from that parent of ten thousand crimes,
The *New Philosophy* of modern times,—
Yet, these may rouse thee!—With unsparing hand,
Oh, lash the vile impostures from the land!

—First, stern Philanthropy:—not she, who dries
The orphan's tears, and wipes the widow's eyes;
Not she, who, sainted Charity her guide,
Of British bounty pours the annual tide;—
But *French* Philanthropy;—whose boundless mind
Glows with the general love of all mankind;—
Philanthropy,—beneath whose baneful sway
Each patriot passion sinks, and dies away.

Taught in her school to imbibe thy mawkish strain,
Condorcet, filter'd through the dregs of Paine,
Each pert adept disowns a Briton's part,
And plucks the name of England from his heart.

What, shall a name, a word, a sound control
The aspiring thought, and cramp the expansive soul?
Shall one half-peopled Island's rocky round
A love, that glows for all Creation, bound?
And social charities contract the plan
Framed for thy Freedom, UNIVERSAL MAN?
—No—through the extended globe his feelings run
As broad and general as the unbounded sun!
No narrow bigot *he*;—*his* reason'd view
Thy interests, England, rank with thine, Peru!
France at our doors, *he* sees no danger nigh,
But heaves for Turkey's woes the impartial sigh;
A steady Patriot of the World alone,
The Friend of every Country—but his own.

Next comes a gentler Virtue.—Ah! beware
Lest the harsh verse her shrinking softness scare.
Visit her not too roughly;—the warm sigh
Breathes on her lips;—the tear-drop gems her eye.
Sweet Sensibility, who dwells enshrined
In the fine foldings of the feeling mind;—
With delicate Mimosa's sense endued,
Who shrinks instinctive from a hand too rude;

Or, like the *anagallis*, prescient flower,
Shuts her soft petals at the approaching shower.

Sweet child of sickly Fancy !—her of yore
From her loved France Rousseau to exile bore ;
And, while midst lakes and mountains wild he ran,
Full of himself, and shunn’d the haunts of man,
Taught her o’er each lone vale and Alpine steep
To lisp the story of his wrongs, and weep ;
Taught her to cherish still in either eye,   ⎫
Of tender tears a plentiful supply,   ⎬
And pour them in the brooks that babbled by ;— ⎭
—Taught by nice scale to meet her feelings strong,
False by degrees, and exquisitely wrong ;—
—For the crush’d beetle *first*,—the widow’d dove,
And all the warbled sorrows of the grove ;—
Next for poor suff’ring *guilt* ;—and *last* of all,
For Parents, Friends, a King and Country’s fall.

Mark her fair votaries, prodigal of grief,
With cureless pangs, and woes that mock relief,
Droop in soft sorrow o’er a faded flower
O’er a dead jack-ass pour the pearly shower ;—
But hear, unmoved, of *Loire’s* ensanguined flood,
Choked up with slain ;—of *Lyons* drench’d in blood ;
Of crimes that blot the age, the world, with shame,
Foul crimes, but sicklied o’er with Freedom’s name ;

Altars and thrones subverted, social life
Trampled to earth,—the husband from the wife,
Parent from child, with ruthless fury torn ;—
Of talents, honour, virtue, wit, forlorn,
In friendless exile,—of the wise and good
Staining the daily scaffold with their blood,—
Of savage cruelties, that scare the mind,
The rage of madness with hell's lust combined—
Of hearts torn reeking from the mangled breast,—
They hear—and hope, that ALL IS FOR THE BEST.

Fond hope !—but JUSTICE sanctifies the pray'r—
JUSTICE !—here, Satire, strike ! 'twere sin to spare !
Not she in British Courts that takes her stand,
The dawdling balance dangling in her hand,
Adjusting punishments to fraud and vice,
With scrupulous quirks, and disquisition nice :—
But firm, erect, with keen reverted glance,
The avenging angel of regenerate France,
Who visits ancient sins on modern times,
And punishes the Pope for Cæsar's crimes.

Such is the liberal JUSTICE which presides
In these our days, and modern patriots guides ;—
JUSTICE, whose blood-stain'd book one sole decree,
One statute fills,—' the People shall be Free.'
Free by what means ?—by folly, madness, guilt,
By boundless rapines, blood in oceans spilt ;

By confiscation, in whose sweeping toils
The poor man's pittance with the rich man's spoils,
Mix'd in one common mass, are swept away,
To glut the short-liv'd tyrant of the day :—
By laws, religion, morals, all o'erthrown ;—
—Rouse then, ye sovereign people, claim your own :—
The licence that enthrals, the truth that blinds,
The wealth that starves you, and the power that grinds.
—So JUSTICE bids.—'Twas her enlighten'd doom,
Louis, thy holy head devoted to the tomb !
'Twas JUSTICE claim'd, in that accursed hour,
The fatal forfeit of too lenient pow'r.
—Mourn for the Man we may ; but for the King,—
Freedom, oh ! Freedom's such a charming thing !

‘ Much may be said on both sides.’—Hark ! I hear
A well-known voice that murmurs in my ear,—
The voice of CANDOUR.—Hail ! most solemn sage,
Thou drivelling virtue of this moral age,
CANDOUR, which softens party's headlong rage.
CANDOUR,—which spares its foes ;—nor e'er descends
With bigot zeal to combat for its friends.
CANDOUR,—which loves in see-saw strain to tell
Of *acting foolishly*, but *meaning well* ;
Too nice to praise by wholesale, or to blame,
Convinced that *all* men's *motives* are the same ;—
And finds, with keen discriminating sight,
BLACK's not *so* black ;—nor WHITE *so very* white.

'Fox, to be sure, was vehement and wrong ;—
But then Pitt's words you'll own were *rather* strong.
Both must be blamed, both pardon'd ;—'twas just so
With Fox and Pitt full forty years ago ;
So Walpole, Pulteney ;—factions in all times,
Have had their follies, ministers their crimes.'

Give me the avow'd, the erect, the manly foe,
Bold I can meet—perhaps may turn his blow ;
But of all plagues, good Heaven, thy wrath can send,
Save, save, oh ! save me from the *Candid Friend !*

'Barras loves plunder,—Merlin takes a bribe,—
What then ?—shall CANDOUR these good men pro-
　　scribe ?
No ! ere we join the loud-accusing throng,
Prove,—not the facts,—but, that *they thought them.
　　wrong.*

'Why hang O'Quigley ?—he, misguided man,
In sober thought his country's weal *might* plan.
And, while his deep-wrought Treason sapp'd the
　　throne,
Might act from *taste in morals* all his own.'

Peace to such Reasoners !—let them have their
　　way ;
Shut their dull eyes against the blaze of day.—

Priestley's a Saint, and Stone a Patriot still !
And La Fayette a Hero, if they will.

I love the bold uncompromising mind,
Whose principles are fix'd, whose views defined :
Who scouts and scorns, in canting CANDOUR's spite,
All *taste in morals*, innate sense of right,
And Nature's impulse, all uncheck'd by art,
And feelings fine, that float about the heart :
Content, for good men's guidance, bad men's awe,
On moral truth to rest, and Gospel law.
Who owns, when Traitors feel the avenging rod,
Just retribution, and the hand of God ;
Who hears the groans through Olmutz' roofs that
          ring,
Of him who mock'd, misled, betray'd his King—
Hears unappall'd :—though Faction's zealots preach—
Unmoved, unsoften'd by F—tzp—tr—ck's speech.
—That speech on which the melting Commons hung,
'While truths divine came mended from *his* tongue'—
How loving husband clings to duteous wife,—
How pure religion soothes the ills of life,—
How Popish ladies trust their pious fears
And naughty actions in their chaplain's ears.—
Half novel and half sermon on it flow'd :
With pious zeal THE OPPOSITION glow'd ;
And as o'er each the soft infection crept,
Sigh'd as he whined, and as he whimper'd wept ;

E'en Curwen dropt a sentimental tear,
And stout Sir A—dr—w yelp'd a softer ' Hear !'

———

O ! nurse of crimes and fashions ! which in vain
Our colder servile spirits would attain,
How do we ape thee, France ! but blundering still
Disgrace the pattern by our want of skill.
The borrow'd step our awkward gait reveals :
(As clumsy C—rtn—y mars the verse he steals.)
How do we ape thee, France !—nor claim alone
Thy arts, thy tastes, thy morals for our own,
But to thy Worthies render homage due,
Their ' hair-breadth 'scapes' with anxious interest view;
Statesmen and heroines whom this age adores,
Tho' plainer times would call them rogues and whores.

See Louvet, patriot, pamphleteer, and sage,
Tempering with amorous fire his virtuous rage.
Form'd for all tasks, his various talents see,—
The luscious novel, the severe decree.
Then mark him weltering in his nasty sty,
Bare his lewd transports to the public eye.
Not *his* the love in silent groves that strays,
Quits the rude world, and shuns the vulgar gaze.
In Lodoiska's full possession blest,
One craving void still aches within his breast ;—
Plunged in the filth and fondness of her arms,
Not to himself alone he stints her charms ;

Clasp'd in each other's foul embrace they lie,
But know no joy, unless the world stands by.
—The fool of vanity, for her alone
He lives, loves, writes, and dies but to be known.

His widow'd mourner flies to poison's aid,
Eager to join her Louvet's parted shade
In those bright realms where sainted lovers stray,—
But harsh emetics tear that hope away.
—Yet hapless Louvet! where thy bones are laid,
The easy nymphs shall consecrate the shade.
There, in the laughing morn of genial spring,
Unwedded pairs shall tender couplets sing;
Eringoes, o'er the hallow'd spot shall bloom,
And flies of Spain buzz softly round the tomb.

But hold, severer virtue claims the Muse—
Roland the just, with ribands in his shoes—
And Roland's spouse who paints with chaste delight
The doubtful conflict of her nuptial night;—
Her virgin charms what fierce attacks assail'd,
And how the rigid Minister prevail'd.

And ah! what verse can grace thy stately mien, ⎫
Guide of the world, preferment's golden queen, ⎬
Neckar's fair daughter,—Stael, the Epicene! ⎭
Bright o'er whose flaming cheek and pumple nose
The bloom of young desire unceasing glows!

Fain would the Muse—but ah ! she dares no more,
A mournful voice from lone Guyana's shore,
—Sad Quatremer—the bold presumption checks,
Forbid to question thy ambiguous sex.

To thee, proud Barras bows ;—thy charms control
Rewbell's brute rage, and Merlin's subtle soul ;
Raised by thy hands, and fashioned to thy will,
Thy power, thy guiding influence, governs still,
Where at the blood-stain'd board expert he plies,
The lame artificer of fraud and lies ;
He with the mitred head and cloven heel ;
Doom'd the coarse edge of Rewbell's jests to feel ;
To stand the playful buffet, and to hear
The frequent ink-stand whizzing past his ear ;
While all the five Directors laugh to see
' The limping priest so deft at his new ministry.'

Last of the ANOINTED FIVE behold, and least,
The Directorial Lama, Sovereign Priest,—
Lepaux :—whom atheists worship ;—at whose nod
Bow their meek heads *the men without a God.*

Ere long, perhaps, to this astonish'd Isle,
Fresh from the shores of subjugated Nile,
Shall Buonaparte's victor fleet protect
The genuine Theo-philanthropic sect,—
The sect of Marat, Mirabeau, Voltaire,—

Led by their Pontiff, good La Reveillère.
—Rejoiced our CLUBS shall greet him, and install
The holy Hunch-back in thy dome, St. Paul!
While countless votaries thronging in his train
Wave their Red Caps, and hymn this jocund strain :

' *Couriers* and *Stars*, Sedition's Evening Host,
Thou *Morning Chronicle*, and *Morning Post*,
Whether ye make the Rights of Man your theme,
Your Country Libel, and your God blaspheme,
Or dirt on private worth and virtue throw,
Still blasphemous or blackguard, praise Lepaux!

' And ye five other wandering Bards, that move
In sweet accord of harmony and love,
C——dge and S—th—y, L—d, and L—b and Co.
Tune all your mystic harps to praise Lepaux!

' Pr—tl—y and W—f—ld, humble, holy men,
Give praises to his name with tongue and pen!

' Th—lw—l, and ye that lecture as ye go,
And for your pains get pelted, praise Lepaux!

' Praise him each Jacobin, or fool, or knave,
And your cropp'd heads in sign of worship wave!

' All creeping creatures, venomous and low,
Paine, W-ll-ms, G-dw-n, H-lcr-ft, praise Lepaux

'⸻ and ⸻ with ⸻ join'd,
And every other beast after his kind.

'And thou, *Leviathan*! on ocean's brim
Hugest of living things that sleep and swim;
Thou, in whose nose by Burke's gigantic hand
The hook was fix'd to drag thee to the land,
With ⸻, ⸻, and ⸻ in thy train,
And ⸻ wallowing in the yeasty main,
Still as ye snort, and puff, and spout, and blow,
In puffing, and in spouting, praise Lepaux!'

Britain, beware; nor let the insidious foe,
Of force despairing, aim a deadlier blow.
Thy peace, thy strength, with devilish wiles assail,
And when her arms are vain, by arts prevail.
True, thou art rich, art powerful!—thro' thine Isle
Industrious skill, contented labour smile;
Far seas are studded with thy countless sails;
What wind but wafts them, and what shore but hails!
True, thou art brave!—o'er all the busy land
In patriot ranks embattled myriads stand;
Thy foes behold with impotent amaze,
And drop the lifted weapon as they gaze!

But what avails to guard each outward part,
If subtlest poison, circling at thy heart,

Spite of thy courage, of thy power, and wealth
Mine the sound fabric of thy vital health ?

So thine own Oak, by some fair streamlet's side
Waves its broad arms, and spreads its leafy pride,
Towers from the earth, and rearing to the skies
Its conscious strength, the tempest's wrath defies :
Its ample branches shield the fowls of air,
To its cool shade the panting herds repair.—
The treacherous current works its noiseless way,—
The fibres loosen, and the roots decay ;
Prostrate the beauteous ruin lies ; and all
That shared its shelter, perish in its fall.
    O thou !—lamented Sage !—whose prescient scan
Pierced through foul Anarchy's gigantic plan,
Prompt to incredulous hearers to disclose
The guilt of France, and Europe's world of woes ;
Thou, on whose name each distant age shall gaze,
The mighty sea-mark of these troubled days !
O large of soul, of genius unconfined,
Born to delight, instruct, and mend mankind ;
Burke ! in whose breast a Roman ardour glowed ;
Whose copious tongue with Grecian richness flow'd ;
Well hast thou found (if such thy Country's doom)
A timely refuge in the sheltering tomb !

As, far in realms, where Eastern kings are laid,
In pomp of death, beneath the cypress shade,

The perfumed lamp with unextinguish'd light
Flames thro' the vault, and cheers the gloom of
    night.—
So, mighty Burke! in thy sepulchral urn,
To fancy's view, the lamp of Truth shall burn.
Thither late times shall turn their reverent eyes,
Led by thy light, and by thy wisdom wise.

There *are*, to whom (*their* taste such pleasures cloy)
No light thy wisdom yields, thy wit no joy.
Peace to their heavy heads, and callous hearts,
Peace—such as sloth, as ignorance imparts!—
Pleased may they live to plan their Country's good,
And crop, with calm content, their flow'ry food!

What though thy venturous spirit loved to urge
The labouring theme to Reason's utmost verge,
Kindling and mounting from the enraptured sight;—
Still anxious wonder watch'd thy daring flight!
—While vulgar minds, with mean malignant stare,
Gazed up, the triumph of thy fall to share!
Poor triumph! price of that extorted praise,
Which still to daring Genius Envy pays.

Oh! for thy playful smile,—thy potent frown,—
To abash bold Vice, and laugh pert folly down!
So should the Muse in Humour's happiest vein,
With verse that flow'd in metaphoric strain,

And apt allusions to the rural trade,
Tell of *what wood young* JACOBINS *are made*;
How the skill'd Gardener grafts with nicest rule
The *slip* of Coxcomb, on the *stock* of fool;
Forth in bright blossom bursts the tender sprig,
A thing to wonder at, perhaps a *Whig*.—
Should tell, how wise each half-fledg'd pedant prates
Of weightiest matters, grave distinctions states—
—That rules of policy, and public good,
In Saxon times were rightly understood;
—That Kings are proper, *may be* useful things,
But then some Gentlemen object to Kings;
—That in all times the Minister's to blame;
—That British Liberty's an empty name,
Till each fair burgh, numerically free,
Shall choose its Members by *the Rule of Three*.

So should the Muse, with verse in thunder clothed,
Proclaim the crimes by God and Nature loath'd.
Which—(when fell poison revels in the veins—
That poison fell, which frantic Gallia drains
From the crude fruit of Freedom's blasted tree)
Blots the fair records of Humanity.

To feebler nations let proud France afford
Her damning choice,—the chalice or the sword,—
To drink or die;—oh fraud! oh specious lie!
Delusive choice! for *if* they drink, they die.

The sword we dread not : of ourselves secure,
Firm were our strength, our Peace and Freedom sure,
Let all the world confederate all its powers,
' Be they not back'd by those that should be ours,'
High on his rock shall BRITAIN'S GENIUS stand,
Scatter the crowded hosts, and vindicate the land.

Guard we but our own hearts : with constant view
To ancient morals, ancient manners true,
True to the manlier virtues, such as nerved
Our fathers' breasts, and this proud Isle preserved
For many a rugged age :—and scorn the while,—
Each philosophic atheist's specious guile—
The soft seductions, the refinements nice,
Of gay morality, and easy vice :
So shall we brave the storm ;—our 'stablish'd power
Thy refuge, Europe, in some happier hour.—
—But, French *in heart*—tho' victory crown our brow,
Low at our feet though prostrate nations bow,
Wealth gild our cities, commerce crowd our shore,—
London may shine, but England is no more.

SIR WALTER SCOTT

(Sir Walter, as he has himself informed us, took little interest in the details of politics: but he sometimes put his poetical faculty at the service of his country or his political party, and the following is, I think, the best result.)

HEALTH TO LORD MELVILLE

1806

SINCE here we are set in array round the table,
   Five hundred good fellows well met in a hall,
Come listen, brave boys, and I'll sing as I'm able
   How innocence triumph'd and pride got a fall.
         But push round the claret—
         Come, stewards, don't spare it—
With rapture you'll drink to the toast that I give :
         Here, boys,
         Off with it merrily—
Melville for ever, and long may he live !

What were the Whigs doing, when boldly pursuing,
  Pitt banish'd Rebellion, gave Treason a sting?
Why, they swore on their honour, for Arthur O'Connor,
  And fought hard for Despard against country and
    king.
        Well, then, we knew, boys,
        Pitt and Melville were true boys,
And the tempest was raised by the friends of Reform.
        Ah, woe!
        Weep to his memory:
Low lies the pilot that weather'd the storm!

And pray, don't you mind when the Blues first were
  raising,
  And we scarcely could think the house safe o'er
    our heads?
When villains and coxcombs, French politics praising,
  Drove peace from our tables and sleep from our
    beds?
        Our hearts they grew bolder
        When, musket on shoulder,
Stepp'd forth our old Statesman example to give.
        Come, boys, never fear,
        Drink the Blue grenadier—
Here's to old Harry, and long may he live!

They would turn us adrift; though rely, sir, upon it—
  Our own faithful chronicles warrant us that

The free mountaineer and his bonny blue bonnet
  Have oft gone as far as the regular's hat.
        We laugh at their taunting,
        For all we are wanting
Is licence our life for our country to give.
        Off with it merrily,
        Horse, foot, and artillery,
Each loyal Volunteer, long may he live.

'Tis not us alone, boys—the Army and Navy
  Have each got a slap 'mid their politic pranks;
Cornwallis cashier'd, that watch'd winters to save ye,
  And the Cape call'd a bauble, unworthy of thanks.
        But vain is their taunt,
        No soldier shall want
The thanks that his country to valour can give:
        Come, boys,
        Drink it off merrily,—
Sir David and Popham, and long may they live!

And then our revenue—Lord knows how they view'd
    it,
  While each petty statesman talk'd lofty and big;
But the beer-tax was weak, as if Whitbread had brew'd
    it,
  And the pig-iron duty a shame to a pig.
        In vain is their vaunting,
        Too surely there's wanting
What judgment, experience, and steadiness give:

Come, boys,
Drink about merrily,—
Health to sage Melville, and long may he live !

Our King, too—our Princess—I dare not say more,
    sir,—
  May Providence watch them with mercy and might !
While there's one Scottish hand that can wag a clay-
    more, sir,
  They shall ne'er want a friend to stand up for their
    right.
Be damn'd he that dare not,—
For my part, I'll spare not
To beauty afflicted a tribute to give :
Fill it up steadily,
Drink it off readily—
Here's to the Princess, and long may she live !

And since we must not set Auld Reekie in glory,
  And make her brown visage as light as her heart ;
Till each man illumine his own upper story,
  Nor law book nor lawyer shall force us to part.
In Grenville and Spencer,
And some few good men, sir,
High talents we honour, slight difference forgive :
But the Brewer we'll hoax,
Tallyho to the Fox,
And drink Melville for ever, as long as we live !

GEORGE CANNING

(*That Canning is the greatest of all political English verse-writers of the lighter kind, as Dryden is of the heavy brigade, is sometimes contested, but not in my judgment contestable. Much of his best work appeared, not always separably, in the* Anti-Jacobin, *which he wrote in conjunction with his friends Ellis, Frere, and others ; but he often equalled the merit of the* Knife-Grinder *and the* New Morality *in his independent work.*)

ANACRÉONTIC

How blest, how firm the statesman stands
(Him no low intrigue can move),
Circled by faithful kindred bands,
　　And propp'd by fond fraternal love.
When his speeches hobble vilely,
What ' Hear hims' burst from Brother Hiley ;

When his falt'ring periods lag,
Hark to the cheers of Brother Bragge ;
When the falt'ring periods lag,
Or the yawning audience flag ;
When his speeches hobble vilely,
Or the House receives them drily,
    Cheer, oh, cheer him, Brother Bragge,
Cheer, oh, cheer him, Brother Hiley.
Each a gentleman at large,
Lodged and fed at public charge,
Paying (with a grace to charm ye),
This the Fleet, and that the Army.
Brother Bragge and Brother Hiley,
Cheer him when he speaks so vilely ;
Cheer him when his audience flag,
Brother Hiley, Brother Bragge.

MODERATE MEN
AND MODERATE MEASURES

PRAISE to placeless proud ability,
    Let the prudent muse disclaim :
And sing the statesman—all civility—
    Whom *moderate talents* raise to fame.
He, no random projects urging,
    Makes us wild alarms to feel ;
With *moderate measures*, gently *purging*
    Ills that prey on Britain's weal.

Chorus

Gently *purging*
Gently *purging*
Gently *purging* Britain's weal.

Addington, with measured *motion,*
  Keep the tenor of thy way;
To glory yield no rash devotion,
  Led by luring lights astray;
Splendid talents are deceiving,
  Tend to counsels much too bold;
Moderate men we prize, believing,
  All that glitters is not gold.

Grand Chorus.

All that *glisters,*
All that *glisters,*
All that *glisters* is not gold!

FRAGMENT OF AN ORATION

I'M like Archimedes for science and skill,
I'm like a young Prince going straight up a hill;
I'm like (with respect to the fair be it said)—
I'm like a young lady just bringing to bed.

If you ask why the 11th of June I remember
Much better than April, or May, or November,
On that day, my Lords, with truth I assure ye,
My sainted progenitor set up his brewery ;
On that day in the morn he began brewing beer,
On that day, too, commenc'd his connubial career ;
On that day he receiv'd and he issued his bills ;
On that day he clear'd out all the cash from his tills ;
On that day he died, having finished his summing,
And the angels all cried, 'Here's old Whitbread a-
    coming.'
So that day still I hail with a smile and a sigh,
For his Beer with an *e* and his Bier with an *i* ;
And still on that day ·in the hottest of weather
The whole Whitbread family dine all together.
So long as the beams of his house shall support
The roof which o'ershades this respectable Court
Where Hastings was tried for oppressing the Hindoos ;
So long as that sun shall shine in at those windows,
My name shall shine bright as my ancestor's shines,
Mine recorded in journals, his blazon'd on signs.

ELIJAH'S MANTLE

A TRIBUTE TO THE MEMORY OF THE RIGHT HON.
WILLIAM PITT

I

WHEN, by th' Almighty's dread command
Elijah, call'd from Israel's land,
    Rose in the sacred flame,
His Mantle good Elisha caught,
And, with the Prophet's spirit fraught,—
    Her second hope became.

II

In Pitt our Israel saw combined
The Patriot's heart—the Prophet's mind,
    Elijah's spirit here:
Now sad reverse !—that spirit reft,
No confidence, no hope is left ;
    For no Elijah's near.

III

Is there, among the greedy band
Who've seized on power, with harpy hand
    And Patriot worth assume,

One on whom public faith can rest—
One fit to wear Elijah's vest,
  And cheer a Nation's gloom?

IV

Grenville !—to aid thy Treasury fame,
A portion of Pitt's Mantle claim,
  His gen'rous ardour feel ;
Resolve, 'bove sordid self to soar,
Amidst Exchequer gold be poor !
  Thy wealth—the public weal.

V

Fox !—if on thee some remnant fall,
The shred may to thy mind recall,
  Those hours of loud debate,
When thy unhallow'd lips be-praised
'The glorious fabric' traitors raised
  On Bourbon's fallen state.

VI

Thy soul let Pitt's example fire,
With patriot zeal thy tongue inspire,
  Spite of thy gallic leaven ;
And teach thee in thy latest day,
His form of prayer (if thou can'st pray),
  'O save my country, Heaven !'

VII

Windham,—if e'er thy sorrows flow
For private loss or public woe,
    Thy rigid brow unbend :
Tears over Cæsar Brutus shed,
His hatred warr'd not with the dead—
    And Pitt was once thy friend.

VIII

Does Envy bid thee not to mourn ?
Hold then his Mantle up to scorn,
    His well-earn'd fame assail :
Of funeral honours strip his corse,
And at his virtues till thou'rt hoarse
    Like curst Thersites rail !

IX

Illustrious Roscius of the State !
New-breech'd and harness'd for debate,
    Thou wonder of thy age !
Petty or Betty thou art hight
By Granta sent to strut thy night
    On Stephen's bustling stage.

X

Pitt's 'Chequer robe 'tis thine to wear ;
Take of his mantle too a share
    'Twill aid thy Ways and Means ;

And should Fat Jack, and his Cabal
Cry 'Rob us the Exchequer, Hal!'
    'Twill charm away the fiends.

XI

Sage Palinurus of the realm!
By Vincent call'd to take the helm!
    And play his proxy's part;
Dost thou or star or compass know?
Can'st reef aloft—or hand below?
      Hast conn'd the shipman's chart?

XII

No!—From Pitt's Mantle tear a rag,
Enough to serve thee for a flag,
    And hoist it on thy mast:
Beneath that sign (our prosperous star)
Shall future Nelsons rush to war,
    And rival victories past.

XIII

Sidmouth—though low his head is laid
Who call'd thee from thy native shade,
    And gave thee second birth;
Gave thee the sweets of Power and Place,
The tufted gown—the gilded mace.
    And rear'd thy puny worth:

XIV

Think how his Mantle wrapp'd thee round :
Is one of equal virtue found
    Among thy new compeers ?
Or can thy cloak of Amiens stuff,
Once laugh'd to scorn by Blue and Buff,
    Screen thee from Windham's jeers ?

XV

When Faction threaten'd Britain's land,
Thy new-made friends—a desperate band,
    Like Ahab—stood reprov'd :
Pitt's powerful tongue their rage could check ;
His counsel sav'd, 'midst general wreck,
    The Israel that he loved.

XVI

Yes, honor'd shade ! whilst near thy grave
The letter'd sage, and chieftain brave,
    The votive marble claim ;
O'er thy cold corse—the public tear
Congeal'd, a crystal shrine shall rear,
    Unsullied as thy fame !

LORD BYRON

(Byron's work would be missed in such a book as this. Therefore I give some of it, though it does not seem to me of the first class.)

SONG FOR THE LUDDITES

As the Liberty lads o'er the sea
Bought their freedom, and cheaply, with blood,
    So we, boys, we
    Will *die* fighting, or *live* free,
And down with all kings but King Ludd !

When the web that we weave is complete,
And the shuttle exchanged for the sword,
    We will fling the winding sheet
    O'er the despot at our feet,
And dye it deep in the gore he has pour'd.

Though black as his heart its hue,
Since his veins are corrupted to mud,
    Yet this is the dew
    Which the tree shall renew
Of Liberty, planted by Ludd!

December 1816.

SONNET TO GEORGE THE FOURTH,

ON THE REPEAL OF LORD EDWARD FITZGERALD'S FORFEITURE

To be the father of the fatherless,
    To stretch the hand from the throne's height,
        and raise
    His offspring, who expired in other days
To make thy sire's sway by a kingdom less,—
This is to be a monarch, and repress
    Envy into unutterable praise.
    Dismiss thy guard, and trust thee to such traits,
For who would lift a hand, except to bless?
    Were it not easy, sir, and is't not sweet
    To make thyself beloved? and to be
Omnipotent by mercy's means? for thus
    Thy sovereignty would grow but more complete;
A despot thou, and yet thy people free,
    And by the heart, not hand, enslaving us.

EPITAPH FOR WILLIAM PITT

WITH death doom'd to grapple,
  Beneath this cold slab, he
Who lied in the Chapel
  Now lies in the Abbey.

EPIGRAM

IN digging up your bones, Tom Paine,
  Will Cobbett has done well:
You visit him on earth again,
  He'll visit you in hell.

STANZAS

WHEN a man hath no freedom to fight for at home,
  Let him combat for that of his neighbours;
Let him think of the glories of Greece and of Rome,
  And get knock'd on the head for his labours.

To do good to mankind is the chivalrous plan,
  And is always as nobly requited;
Then battle for freedom wherever you can,
  And, if not shot or hang'd, you'll get knighted.

N

THOMAS MOORE

(Something has been said of Moore's political verse in the Introduction. It is extraordinarily good, and it distinctly improved as he went on. Metrical faculty and ready wit, the two qualities most required by the political bard, he possessed in abundance, and the result is charming.)

THE EXTINGUISHERS

PROEM

THOUGH soldiers are the true supports,
The natural allies of Courts,
Woe to the Monarch who depends
Too *much* on his red-coated friends;
For even soldiers sometimes think—
    Nay Colonels have been known to *reason*,—
And reasoners, whether clad in pink,
Or red, or blue, are on the brink
    (Nine cases out of ten) of treason.

Not many soldiers, I believe, are
  As fond of liberty as Mina ;
Else—woe to Kings, when Freedom's fever
  Once turns into a *Scarlatina* !
For then—but hold—'tis best to veil
My meaning in the following tale :—

FABLE

A LORD of Persia, rich and great,
Just come into a large estate,
Was shocked to find he had, for neighbours,
Close to his gate, some rascal Ghebers,
Whose fires, beneath his very nose,
In heretic combustion rose.
But lords of Persia can, no doubt,
  Do what they will—so, one fine morning,
He turned the rascal Ghebers out,
  First giving a few kicks for warning.
Then, thanking Heaven most piously,
  He knocked their temple to the ground,
Blessing himself for joy to see
  Such Pagan ruins strewed around.
But much it vexed my lord to find,
  That, while all else obeyed his will,
The fire these Ghebers left behind—
  Do what he would—kept burning still.

Fiercely he stormed, as if his frown
Could scare the bright insurgent down ;
But, no—such fires are headstrong things,
And care not much for lords or kings.
Scarce could his lordship well contrive
   The flashes in *one* place to smother,
Before—hey, presto !—all alive,
   They sprung up freshly in another.

At length, when, spite of prayers and damns,
   'Twas found the sturdy flame defied him,
His stewards came, with low *salams*,
   Offering, by *contract*, to provide him
Some large extinguishers (a plan
Much used, they said, at Ispahan,
Vienna, Petersburgh—in short
Wherever light's forbid at court)—
Machines no lord should be without,
Which would, at once, put promptly out
Fires of all kinds—from staring stark
Volcanos to the tiniest spark—
Till all things slept as dull and dark
As, in a great lord's neighbourhood,
'Twas right and fitting all things should.

Accordingly, some large supplies
   Of these extinguishers were furnished
(All of the true, imperial size),

And there, in rows, stood black and burnished,
Ready, where'er a gleam but shone
Of light or fire, to be clapped on.

But, ah! how lordly wisdom errs
In trusting to extinguishers!
One day, when he had left all sure
(At least *believed* so), dark, secure—
The flame, at all its exits, entries,
　　Obstructed to his heart's content,
And black extinguishers, like sentries,
　　Placed upon every dangerous vent—
Ye Gods! imagine his amaze,
　　His wrath, his rage, when, on returning,
He found not only the old blaze,
　　Brisk as before, crackling and burning—
Not only new, young conflagrations,
Popping up round in various stations—
But, still more awful, strange, and dire,
The extinguishers themselves on fire!!
They, they—those trusty, blind machines
　　His lordship had so long been praising,
As, under Providence, the means
　　Of keeping down all lawless blazing,
Were now themselves—alas, too true
The shameful fact!—turned blazers too,
And, by a change as odd as cruel,
Instead of dampers, served for fuel!

Thus, of his only hope bereft,
  'What,' said the great man, 'must be done?'
All that, in scrapes like this, is left
  To great men is—to cut and run.
So run he did; while to their grounds
  The banished Ghebers blessed returned;
And, though their fire had broke its bounds,
  And all abroad now wildly burned,
Yet well could they, who loved the flame,
Its wandering, its excess reclaim;
And soon another, fairer dome
Arose to be its sacred home,
Where, cherished, guarded, not confined,
The living glory dwelt enshrined,
And, shedding lustre, strong but even,
Though born of earth, grew worthy Heaven.

MORAL

The moral hence my Muse infers
  Is—that such lords are simple elves,
In trusting to extinguishers
  That are combustible themselves.

THE TWOPENNY POST-BAG

LETTER I

FROM THE PR——NC——SS CH————E OF W——S TO
THE LADY B——RB——A A——SHL——Y

My dear Lady Bab, you'll be shocked, I'm afraid,
When you hear the sad rumpus your ponies have
     made ;
Since the time of horse-consuls (now long out of
     date)
No nags ever made such a stir in the State !

Lord Eld——n first heard——and as instantly prayed he
To God and his King——that a Popish young lady
(For though you've bright eyes, and twelve thousand
     a year,
It is still but too true you're a Papist, my dear)
Had insidiously sent, by a tall Irish groom,
Two priest-ridden ponies, just landed from Rome,
And so full, little rogues, of pontifical tricks,
That the dome of St. Paul's was scarce safe from
     their kicks !

Off at once to papa, in a flurry, he flies—
For papa always does what these statesmen advise,
On condition that they'll be, in turn so polite
As in no case whate'er to advise him *too right*—
' Pretty doings are here, sir' (he angrily cries,
While by dint of dark eyebrows he strives to look
    wise);
' 'Tis a scheme of the Romanists, so help me God!
To ride over your most Royal Highness roughshod—
Excuse, sir, my tears, they're from loyalty's source—
Bad enough 'twas for Troy to be sacked by a *Horse*,
But for us to be ruined by *Ponies*, still worse!'

Quick a council is called—the whole cabinet sits—
The Archbishops declare, frightened out of their wits,
That if vile Popish ponies should eat at my manger,
From that awful moment the Church is in danger!
As, give them but stabling, and shortly no stalls
Will suit their proud stomachs but those of St. Paul's.

    The Doctor, and he, the devout man of Leather,
V—ns—tt—t, now laying their saint-heads together,
Declare that these skittish young *a*-bominations
Are clearly foretold in chap. vi. Revelations—
Nay, they verily think they could point out the one
Which the Doctor's friend Death was to canter upon!

Lord H—rr—by, hoping that no one imputes
To the Court any fancy to persecute brutes,

Protests, on the word of himself and his cronies,
That had these said creatures been Asses, not Ponies,
The Court would have started no sort of objection,
As Asses were, *there*, always sure of protection.

'If the Pr—nc—ss *will* keep them (says Lord
    C—stl—r—gh),
To make them quite harmless, the only true way
Is (as certain Chief-Justices do with their wives)
To flog them within half an inch of their lives—
If they've any bad Irish blood lurking about,
This (he knew by experience) would soon draw it
    out.'
Or—if this be thought cruel—his Lordship proposes
'The new *Veto*-snaffle to bind down their noses—
A pretty contrivance, made out of old chains,
Which appears to indulge, while it doubly restrains ;
Which, however high-mettled, their gamesomeness
    checks
(Adds his Lordship humanely), or else breaks their
    necks !'

This proposal received pretty general applause
From the statesmen around—and the neck-breaking
    clause
Had a vigour about it, which soon reconciled
Even Eld—n himself to a measure so mild.
So the snaffles, my dear, were agreed to nem. con.,

And my lord C—stl—r—gh, having so often shone
In the *fettering* line, is to buckle them on.

I shall drive to your door in these *Vetos* some day,
But, at present, adieu!—I must hurry away
To go see my mamma, as I'm suffered to meet her
For just half-an-hour by the Q—n's best repeater.

C——E.

KING CRACK AND HIS IDOLS

WRITTEN AFTER THE LATE NEGOCIATION FOR A NEW M—N—STRY

KING CRACK was the best of all possible Kings
  (At least, so his courtiers would swear to you
    gladly),
But Crack now and then would do het'rodox things,
  And, at last, took to worshipping *Images* sadly.

Some broken-down Idols, that long had been placed
  In his Father's old *Cabinet*, pleased him so much,
That he knelt down and worshipp'd, though—such
    was his taste !—
    They were monstrous to look at, and rotten to
    touch !

And these were the beautiful Gods of King Crack!—
 Till his people, disdaining to worship such things,
Cried aloud, one and all, 'Come, your Godships
  must pack—
 You will not do for *us*, though you *may* do for
  Kings.'

Then, trampling the gross Idols under their feet,
 They sent Crack a petition, beginning 'Great
  Cæsar!
We are willing to worship, but only entreat
 That you'll find us some *decenter* Godheads than
  these are.'

'I'll try,' says King Crack—then they furnish'd him
  models
 Of better-shaped Gods, but he sent them all back;
Some were chisell'd too fine, some had heads 'stead
  of noddles,
 In short, they were all *much* too godlike for Crack!

So he took to his darling old Idols again,
 And, just mending their legs, and new bronzing
  their faces
In open defiance of Gods and of men,
 Set the monsters up grinning once more in their
  places!

LINES

ON THE DEATH OF MR. P—R—V—L

In the dirge we sung o'er him no censure was heard,
　Unembittered and free did the tear-drop descend;
We forgot in that hour how the statesman had erred,
　And wept, for the husband, the father and friend.

Oh! proud was the meed his integrity won,
　And generous indeed were the tears that we shed,
When in grief we forgot all the ill he had done,
　And, though wronged by him living, bewailed him
　　when dead.

Even now, if one harsher emotion intrude,
　'Tis to wish he had chosen some lowlier state—
Had known what he was, and, content to be *good*,
　Had ne'er for our ruin aspired to be *great.*

So, left through their own little orbit to move,
　His years might have rolled inoffensive away;
His children might still have been blessed with his
　　love,
　And England would ne'er have been cursed with
　　his sway.

THE CONSULTATION

'When they *do* agree, their unanimity is wonderful.'—*The Critic.*

Scene discovers DR. WHIG *and* DR. TORY *in consultation. Patient on the floor between them.*

DR. WHIG.—This wild Irish patient *does* pester me so,
That what to do with him, I'm curst if I know ;
I've *promis'd* him anodynes——
    DR. TORY.   Anodynes !—Stuff.
Tie him down—gag him well—he'll be tranquil enough.
That's *my* mode of practice.
    DR. WHIG.   True, quite in *your* line,
But unluckily not much, till lately, in *mine.*
'Tis so painful——
    DR. TORY.—Pooh, nonsense—ask Ude how he feels,
When, for Epicure feasts, he prepares his live eels,
By flinging them in, 'twixt the bars of the fire,
And letting them wriggle on there till they tire.
He, too, says ''tis painful'—'quite makes his heart bleed '——
But 'your eels are a vile, oleaginous breed.'——

He would fain use them gently, but Cookery says
   'No,'
And—in short—eels were *born* to be treated just so.
'Tis the same with these Irish,—who're odder fish
   still,—
Your tender Whig heart shrinks from using them ill;
I, myself, in my youth, ere I came to get wise,
Used, at some operations, to blush to the eyes;—
But, in fact, my dear brother,—if I may make bold
To style you, as Peachum did Lockit of old,—
We, Doctors, *must* act with the firmness of Ude,
And, indifferent like him,—so the fish is *but* stew'd,—
Must torture live Pats for the general good.

       [*Here patient groans and kicks a little.*

  Dr. Whig.—But what, if one's patient's so devilish
    perverse,
That he *won't* be thus tortur'd?
  Dr. Tory.   Coerce, sir, coerce.
You're a juvenile performer, but once you begin,
You can't think how fast you may train your hand in:
And (*smiling*) who knows but old Tory may take to
    the shelf,
With the comforting thought that, in place and in
    pelf,
He's succeeded by one just as— bad as himself?
  Dr. Whig (*looking flattered*).—Why, to tell you the
    truth, I've a small matter here,

Which you help'd me to make for my patient last
    year,—

    [*Goes to cupboard and brings out a strait waist-
       coat and gag.*

And such rest I've enjoyed from his raving since
    then,
That I have made up my mind he shall wear it again.
    Dr. Tory (*embracing him*).—Oh, charming! My
    dear Doctor Whig, you're a treasure.
Next to torturing *myself*, to help *you* is a pleasure.

           [*Assisting* Dr. Whig.

Give me leave — I've some practice in these mad
    machines ;
There—tighter—the gag in the mouth, by all means.
Delightful! all's snug—not a squeak need you fear,—
You may now put your anodynes off till next year.

           [*Scene closes.*

PADDY'S METAMORPHOSIS

About fifty years since, in the days of our daddies,
    That plan was commenc'd which the wise now
    applaud,
Of shipping off Ireland's most turbulent Paddies,
    As good raw materials for *settlers*, abroad.

Some West Indian island, whose name I forget,
 Was the region then chosen for this scheme so
  romantic ;
And such the success the first colony met,
 That a second, soon after, set sail o'er th' Atlantic.

Behold them now safe at the long-look'd for shore,
 Sailing in between banks that the Shannon might
  greet,
And thinking of friends whom, but two years before,
 They had sorrow'd to lose, but would soon again
  meet.

And, hark ! from the shore a glad welcome there
  came—
 ' Arrah, Paddy from Cork, is it you, my sweet
  boy ? '
While Pat stood astounded, to hear his own name
 Thus hail'd by black devils, who caper'd for joy !

Can it possibly be ?—half amazement—half doubt,
 Pat listens again—rubs his eyes and looks steady ;
Then heaves a deep sigh, and in horror yells out,
 ' Good Lord ! only think—black and curly already!'

Deceiv'd by that well-mimick'd brogue in his ears,
 Pat read his own doom in these wool-headed
  figures,

And thought, what a climate, in less than two years,
  To turn a whole cargo of Pats into niggers!

MORAL

'Tis thus,—but alas!—by a marvel more true
  Than is told in this rival of Ovid's best stories,—
Your Whigs, when in office a short year or two,
  By a *lusus naturæ*, all turn into Tories.

And thus, when I hear them 'strong measures'
    advise,
  Ere the seats that they sit on have time to get
    steady,
I say, while I listen, with tears in my eyes,
  'Good Lord!—only think,—black and curly
    already!'

THE SONG OF THE BOX

LET History boast of her Romans and Spartans,
  And tell how they stood against tyranny's shocks;
They were all, I confess, in *my* eye, Betty Martins,
  Compar'd to George Gr—te and his wonderful
  Box.

O

Ask, where Liberty now has her seat?—Oh, it isn't
    By Delaware's banks or on Switzerland's rocks ;—
Like an imp in some conjuror's bottle imprison'd,
    She's slily shut up in Gr—te's wonderful Box.

How snug!—'stead of floating through ether's do-
    minions,
    Blown *this* way and *that*, by the ' populi vox,'
To fold thus in silence her sinecure pinions,
    And go fast asleep in Gr—te's wonderful Box.

Time was, when free speech was the life-breath of
    freedom—
    So thought once the Seldens, the Hampdens, the
        Lockes ;
But mute be *our* troops, when to ambush we lead
    'em,
    For 'Mum' is the word with us Knights of the
        Box.

Pure, exquisite Box! no corruption can soil it ;
    There's Otto of Rose, in each breath it unlocks ;
While Gr—te is the ' Betty,' that serves at the toilet,
    And breathes all Arabia around from his Box.

'Tis a singular tact, that the fam'd Hugo Grotius
    (A namesake of Gr—te's—being both of Dutch
        stocks),

Like Gr—te, too, a genius profound as precocious,
  Was also, like him, much renown'd for a Box ;—

An immortal old clothes-box in which the great
    Grotius
  When suffering, in prison, for views heterodox,
Was pack'd up incog., spite of gaolers ferocious,
  And sent to his wife, carriage free, in a Box !

But the fame of old Hugo now rests on the shelf,
  Since a rival hath ris'n that all parallel mocks ;—
That Grotius ingloriously sav'd but himself,
  While *ours* saves the whole British realm by a
    Box !

And oh, when at last, even this greatest of Gr—tes
  Must bend to the Power that at every door knocks,
May he drop in the urn like his own 'silent votes,'
  And the tomb of his rest be a large Ballot-Box.

While long at his shrine, both from country and city,
  Shall pilgrims triennially gather in flocks,
And sing, while they whimper, th' appropriate ditty,
  'Oh breathe not his *name*, let it sleep—in the Box.'

A CHARACTER

HALF Whig, half Tory, like those midway things,
'Twixt bird and beast, that by mistake have wings ;
A mongrel Statesman, 'twixt two factions nurst,
Who, of the faults of each, combines the worst—
The Tory's loftiness, the Whigling's sneer,
The leveller's rashness, and the bigot's fear ;
The thirst for meddling, restless still to show
How Freedom's clock, repair'd by Whigs, will go ;
Th' alarm when others, more sincere than they,
Advance the hands to the true time of day.

By Mother Church, high-fed and haughty dame,
The boy was dandled, in his dawn of fame ;
List'ning, she smil'd, and bless'd the flippant tongue
On which the fate of unborn tithe-pigs hung.
Ah, who shall paint the grandam's grim dismay,
When loose Reform entic'd her boy away ;
When shock'd she heard him ape the rabble's tone,
And, in Old Sarum's fate, foredoom her own !
Groaning she cried, while tears roll'd down her
    cheeks,
'Poor glib-tongued youth, he means not what he
    speaks.

Like oil at top, these Whig professions flow,
But, pure as lymph, runs Toryism below.
Alas, that tongue should start thus in the race,
Ere mind can reach and regulate its pace !—
For, once outstripp'd by tongue, poor, lagging mind,
At every step, still further limps behind.
But, bless the boy !—whate'er his wandering be,
Still turns his heart to Toryism and me.
Like those odd shapes, portray'd in Dante's lay,
With heads fix'd on, the wrong and backward way,
His feet and eyes pursue a diverse track,
While *those* march onward, *these* look fondly back.'
And well she knew him—well foresaw the day,
Which now hath come, when snatch'd from Whigs
     away,
The self-same changeling drops the mask he wore,
And rests, restor'd in granny's arms once more.

But whither now, mixt brood of modern light
And ancient darkness, can'st thou bend thy flight ?
Tried by both factions, and to neither true,
Fear'd by the *old* school, laugh'd at by the *new* ;
For *this* too feeble, and for *that* too rash,
This wanting more of fire, *that* less of flash ;
Lone shalt thou stand, in isolation cold,
Betwixt two worlds, the new one and the old,
A small and ' vex'd Bermoothes,' which the eye
Of venturous seaman sees—and passes by.

EPISTLE FROM HENRY OF EXETER TO JOHN OF TUAM

DEAR John, as I know, like our brother of London,
You've sipp'd of all knowledge, both sacred and
    mundane,
No doubt, in some ancient Joe Miller, you've read
What Cato, that cunning old Roman, once said—
That he ne'er saw two rev'rend soothsayers meet,
Let it be where it might, in the shrine or the street,
Without wondering the rogues, 'mid their solemn
    grimaces,
Didn't burst out a laughing in each other's faces.
What Cato then meant, though 'tis so long ago,
Even we in the present times pretty well know;
Having soothsayers also, who—sooth to say, John—
Are no better in some points than those of days
    gone,
And a pair of whom meeting (between you and me),
Might laugh in their sleeves, too—all lawn though
    they be.
But this, by the way—my intention being chiefly
In this, my first letter, to hint to you briefly,
That, seeing how fond you of *Tuum* must be,
While *Meum* 's at all times the main point with me,
We scarce could do better than form an alliance,

To set these sad Anti-Church times at defiance :
You, John, recollect, being still to embark,
With no share in the firm but your title and *mark* ;
Or ev'n should you feel in your grandeur inclin'd
To call yourself Pope, why, I shouldn't much mind ;
Why *my* church as usual holds fast by your Tuum,
And every one else's, to make it all Suum.

Thus allied, I've no doubt we shall nicely agree,
As no twins can be liker, in most points than we ;
Both, specimens choice of that mix'd sort of beast,
(See Rev. xiii. 1) a political priest ;
Both meddlesome *chargers*, both brisk pamphleteers,
Ripe and ready for all that sets men by the ears ;
And I, at least one, who would scorn to stick longer
By any giv'n cause than I found it the stronger,
And who, smooth on my turnings as if on a swivel,
When the tone ecclesiastic won't do, try the *civil*.

In short (not to bore you, ev'n *jure divino*)
We've the same cause in common, John—all but the
    rhino ;
And that vulgar surplus, whate'er it may be,
As you're not us'd to cash, John, you'd best leave to
    me.
And so, without form—as the postman won't tarry—
I'm, dear Jack of Tuam,
                                    Yours,
                                    EXETER HARRY.

REFLECTIONS

ADDRESSED TO THE AUTHOR OF THE ARTICLE ON
THE CHURCH, IN THE LAST NUMBER OF THE
' QUARTERLY REVIEW '

I'M quite of your mind ;—though these Pats cry
    aloud
  That they've got ' too much Church,' 'tis all non-
    sense and stuff ;
For Church is like Love, of which Figaro vow'd
  That even *too much* of it's not quite enough.

Ay, dose them with parsons, 'twill cure all their
    ills ;—
  Copy Morison's mode when from pill-box un-
    daunted he
Pours through his patient his black-coated pills,
  Nor cares what their quality, so there's but
    quantity.

I verily think, 'twould be worth England's while
  To consider, for Paddy's own benefit, whether
'Twould not be as well to give up the green isle
  To the care, wear and tear of the Church alto-
    gether.

The Irish are well us'd to treatment so pleasant;
    The harlot Church gave them to Henry Plan-
        tagenet,
And now, if King William would make them a
    present
    To 'tother chaste lady—ye Saints, just imagine it !

Chief Secs., Lord-Lieutenants, Commanders in chief,
    Might then be all cull'd from th' episcopal benches;
While colonels in black would afford some relief
    From the hue that reminds one of th' old scarlet
    wench's.

Think how fierce at a *charge* (being practis'd therein)
    The Right Reverend Brigadier Ph—ll—tts would
    slash on !
How General Bl—mf—d, through thick and through
    thin,
    To the end of the chapter (or chapters) would
    dash on !

For, in one point alone do the amply fed race
    Of bishops to beggars similitude bear—
That, set them on horseback, in full steeple chase,
    And they'll ride, if not pull'd up in time—you
    know where.

But, bless you, in Ireland, that matters not much,
    Where affairs have for centuries gone the same
        way;
And a good staunch Conservative's system is such
    That he'd back even Beelzebub's long-founded
        sway.

I am therefore, dear Quarterly, quite of your mind ;—
    Church, Church, in all shapes, into Erin let's pour ;
And the more she rejecteth our med'cine so kind,
    The more let's repeat it—'Black dose, as before.'

Let Coercion, that peace-maker, go hand in hand
    With demure-ey'd Conversion, fit sister and brother;
And, covering with prisons and churches the land,
    All that won't *go* to *one*, we'll put *into* the other.

For the sole, leading maxim of us who're inclin'd
    To rule over Ireland, not well, but religiously,
Is to treat her like ladies, who've just been confin'd,
    (Or who *ought* to be so) and to *church* her pro-
        digiously.

RELIGION AND TRADE

'Sir Robert Peel believed it was necessary to originate all re-
specting religion and trade in a Committee of the House.'
—*Church Extension*, May 22, 1830.

SAY, who was the wag, indecorously witty,
  Who, first in a statute, this libel convey'd;
And thus slily referr'd to the self-same committee,
  As matters congenial, Religion and Trade?

Oh surely, my Ph—llp—ts, 'twas thou did the deed;
  For none but thyself, or some pluralist brother,
Accustom'd to mix up the craft with the creed,
  Could bring such a pair thus to twin with each
    other.

And yet, when one thinks of times present and gone,
  One is forc'd to confess, on maturer reflection,
That 'tisn't in the eyes of committees alone
  That the shrine and the shop seem to have some
    connection.

Not to mention those monarchs of Asia's fair land,
  Whose civil list all is in 'god-money' paid;
And where the whole people by royal command,
  Buy their gods at the government mart ready
    made;—

There was also (as mention'd, in rhyme and in prose,
 is)
Gold heap'd, throughout Egypt, on every shrine,
To make rings for right reverend crocodiles' noses—
 Just such as, my Ph—llp—ts, would look well in
  thine.

But one needn't fly off, in this erudite mood;
 And 'tis clear, without going to regions so sunny,
That priests love to do the *least* possible good,
 For the largest *most* possible quantum of money.

'Of him,' saith the text, 'unto whom much is given,
 Of him much, in turn, will be also requir'd:'—
'By *me*,' quoth the sleek and obese man of heaven—
 'Give as much as you will—more will still be
  desir'd.'

More money! more churches!—oh Nimrod, hadst
 thou
'Stead of *Tower*-extension, some shorter way gone—
Hadst thou known by what methods we mount to
 heaven *now*,
 And tried *Church*-extension, the feat had been
  done.

WINTHROP MACKWORTH PRAED

(What has been said of Moore may be repeated almost verbatim of Praed, who, with a sufficient difference of education, circumstances, and temperament, employed the same gifts on (for the most part) the other side. As Catholic emancipation and coercion in Ireland were Moore's great themes, so reform and the vagaries of the early reformed parliaments were Praed's.)

ODE TO THE CHANCELLOR

IMITATED FROM HORACE, LIB. III. OD. XV.

OLD Lady of Chancery, why do you tarry
  So long on the throne of your vanishing reign?
The neighbourhood titters whene'er you miscarry,
  And hints that your labours are labours in vain.

There is one thing at least, which your closest
    endeavour
  Will hardly discover a reason to doubt,

That be Candles and Statesmen how wicked soever,
    All Candles and Statesmen at last must go out.

When girls in their summer begin to grow willing,
    Their grandmothers think about making their wills;
And oh! you had better have done with your billing,
    Before your old lovers say 'no,' to your bills.

'Tis all very pretty, when love or defiance
    Is breathed from the lips of a younger coquette;
When Peel is seduced by the Holy Alliance,
    Or Robinson flirts with the National Debt;

But it is not for you, while the grave gapes before you,
    To be scaring gilt stars with those wrinkles of awe;
Giving garter and ribbons to fools who adore you,
    And stealing silk gowns from your daughters-in-law.

Sweet Gifford, I grant, as your tenderness taught her,
    May flaunt in rich suits, and be kind to Appeals;
And dabble her scull in the dirtiest water,
    Like a Greenlander, all for the love of the Seals;

But you—put your salary up in your full sack,
    And go to your grave with a gentle decline;
Take a nightcap of woollen instead of a woolsack,
    And leave to George Canning his roses and wine.

EPITAPH

ON THE LATE KING OF THE SANDWICH ISLANDS.
TRANSLATED FROM THE ORIGINAL OF CRAZEE
RATTEE, HIS MAJESTY'S POET LAUREATE.

BENEATH this marble, mud, or moss,
    Whiche'er his subjects shall determine,
Entombed in eulogies and dross, ˑ
    The Island King is food for vermin :
Preserved by scribblers, and by salt,
    From Lethe, and sepulchral vapours,
His body fills his fathers' vault,
    His character, the daily papers.

Well was he framed for royal seat ;
    Kind to the meanest of his creatures,
With tender heart, and tender feet,
    And open purse, and open features;
The ladies say, who laid him out,
    And earned thereby the usual pensions,
They never wreathed a shroud about
    A corpse of more genteel dimensions.

He warred with half a score of foes,
    And shone, by proxy in the quarrel ;

Enjoyed hard fights, and soft repose,
    And deathless debt, and deathless laurel :
His enemies were scalped and flayed,
    Where'er his soldiers were victorious ;
And widows wept, and paupers paid,
    To make their Sovereign Ruler glorious.

And days were set apart for thanks,
    And prayers were said by pious readers,
And land was lavished on the ranks,
    And land was lavished on their leaders ;
Events are writ by History's pen,
    And causes are too much to care for ;
Fame talks about the where and when,
    While Folly asks the why and wherefore.

In peace he was immensely gay,
    And indefatigably busy ;
Preparing gew-gaws every day,
    And shows to make his subjects dizzy ;
And hearing the reports of guns,
    And signing the reports of gaolers ;
And making up recipes for buns,
    And patterns for the army tailors ;

And building carriages, and boats,
    And streets, and chapels, and pavilions ;
And regulating all the coats,
    And all the principles of millions ;

And drinking homilies and gin,
    And chewing pork and adulation;
And looking backwards upon sin,
    And looking forwards to salvation.

The people in his happy reign,
    Were blest beyond all other nations,
Unharmed by foreign axe or chain,
    Unhealed by civil innovations :
They served the usual logs and stones,
    With all the usual rights and terrors;
And swallowed all their fathers' bones,
    And swallowed all their fathers' errors.

When a fierce mob with clubs and knives,
    Declared that nothing would content them,
But that their representatives
    Should actually represent them,
He interposed the proper checks,
    By sending troops with drums and banners,
Cut short their speeches, and their necks,
    And broke their heads, to mend their manners.

And when Dissension flung her stain
    Upon the light of Hymen's altar,
And Destiny made Cupid's chain
    As galling as the hangman's halter,

P

He passed a most domestic life,
　By many mistresses befriended :
And did not put away his wife,
　For fear the Priests should be offended.

And thus at last he sunk to rest
　Amid the blessings of his people ;
And sighs were heaved from every breast,
　And bells wore tolled from every steeple ;
And loud was every public throng,
　His brilliant character adorning ;
And poets raised a mourning song,
　And clothiers raised the price of mourning.

His funeral was very grand,
　Followed by many robes and maces,
And all the great ones of the land,
　Struggling, as heretofore, for places.
And every loyal Minister
　Was there with signs of purse-felt sorrow,
Save Pozzy, his Lord Chancellor,
　Who promised to attend to-morrow.

Peace to his dust ! his fostering care ;
　By grateful hearts shall long be cherished ;
And all his subjects shall declare,
　They lost a grinder, when he perished.

They who shall look upon the lead,
   In which a people's love hath shrined him,
Shall say, when all the worst is said,
   Perhaps he leaves a worse behind him !

WATERLOO

' It was here that the French cavalry charged, and cut to pieces the English squares.'—*Narrative of a French Tourist.*

' Is it true, think you ? '—*Winter's Tale.*

I

Ay, here such valorous deeds were done
   As ne'er were done before ;
Ay, here the reddest wreath was won
   That ever Gallia wore :
Since Ariosto's wondrous knight
   Made all the Pagans dance,
There never dawned a day so bright
   As Waterloo's on France.

II

The trumpet poured its deafening sound—
   Flags fluttered on the gale ;

And cannon roared, and heads flew round
    As fast as summer hail :
The sabres flashed ; with rage and fear
    The steeds began to prance ;
The English quaked from front to rear,—
    They never quake in France !

III

The cuirassiers rode in and out,
    As fierce as wolves and bears ;
'Twas grand to see them slash about
    Among the English squares !
And then the Polish lancer came,
    Careering with his lance ;—
No wonder Britain blushed for shame,
    And ran away from France.

IV

The Duke of York was killed that day—
    The King was sadly scarred ;—
Lord Eldon, as he ran away,
    Was taken by the Guard.
Poor Wellington, with fifty Blues,
    Escaped by some strange chance ;
Henceforth, I think he'll hardly choose
    To show himself in France.

V

So Buonaparte pitched his tent
    That day in Grosvenor Place;
And Ney rode straight to Parliament,
    And broke the Speaker's mace.
'Vive l'Empereur' was said or sung,
    From Peebles to Penzance;
The Mayor and Aldermen were hung,
    Which made folks laugh in France.

VI

They pulled the Tower of London down;
    They burned our wooden walls;
They brought his Holiness to Town,
    And lodged him in St. Paul's.
And Gog and Magog rubbed their eyes,
    Awaking from a trance;
And grumbled out, in great surprise,
    'O mercy! we're in France!'

VII

They sent a Regent to our Isle,—
    The little King of Rome;
And squibs and crackers all the while
    Blazed in the Place Vendome.

And ever since, in arts and power
   They're making great advance ;
They've had strong beer from that glad·hour,
   And sea-coal fires in France.

VIII

My uncle, Captain Flanigan,
   Who lost a leg in Spain,
Tells stories of a little man,
   Who died at St. Helène.
But bless my heart ! they can't be true,
   I'm sure they're all romance ;
John Bull was beat at Waterloo—
   They'll swear to that in France !

THE COMPLAINT OF LIBERTY

'Lord,' said the Little Woman, 'sure it can't be I !'—
Old Song.

'Oh, Liberty, whose radiant charms
   Were so adored by Thebes and Sparta,
Bright patroness of arts and arms,
   And authoress of Magna Charta,—
Nymph, for whose sake, as we are taught
   In Plutarch's entertaining stories,

Speeches were made, and battles fought,
　By Greek and Roman Whigs and Tories.

'Come hither, with your pen and sword,
　Your russet garb, your mess of pottage;
Leave the wild Arab's wandering horde,
　Or the rude Switzer's humble cottage;
Let Lafayette console Lafitte;
　Let Congress sit a day without you;
Smile, smile, for once, on Downing-street;
　I want to write an ode about you.'

She came; she answered!—Well I know
　The Speaker's awful call to order;
I heard, some thirteen years ago,
　A sentence from the late Recorder;
I know how hoarse the cheerers are
　When Whig Lords talk of right intention;
But oh, that fearful voice was far
　More fearful than the sounds I mention.

'I come,' she said, 'the same who erst
　Held talk with Xenophon and Plato;
Taught Brutus to be firm, and merst
　The fire of high resolve in Cato:
The same, who on your island rock
　Have mock'd the hand of sceptred power;
Who went with Sydney to the block,
　And with the Bishops to the Tower.

' Alas ! my handmaids in such days
　　Were Wisdom, Order, and Sobriety.
What loathsome change !—my Broughams and Greys
　　Have dragged me into strange society ;
Treason and strife invoke my name
　　In their dark plots and drunken quarrels ;
I'm growing weary of my fame ;
　　And, Jove ! how ill I look in laurels.

'Calcraft is dozing in my lap,
　　Which surely is a shocking scandal ;
The Chancellor has curled my cap,
　　And Henry Hunt has blacked my sandal ;
I run with Murphys and O'Shanes
　　To ruin some unhappy banker ;
And Hobhouse sets me breaking chains
　　For Poland, at the Crown and Anchor.

' I am not what I was !　I throw
　　Prodigious stones in Clare and Kerry ;
I cheat the Greeks with prudent Joe ;
　　I maximise with sapient Jerry :
Last winter, I confess, I taught
　　The labouring class the art of arson ;
And oft, on Sundays, I've been caught
　　With Taylor, screaming out, " No Parson ! "

' It's true that still the schoolboy's prayers,
　　Come up to me in so-so Latin ;

And still the lying *Courier* swears
   The rags I wear are silk and satin :
And I've a friend at Court, I think,
   But he will doom me to the halter,
When once he hears me, in my drink,
   Speak out about the throne and altar.

   'Farewell ! my anguish would defy
      E'en Althorp's powers of clear expression ;
I'm quite convinced that I shall die
      Before the closing of the Session !
I'd go with pleasure to the Grave,
      But oh ! the thought is overpowering ;
They tell me I am sure to have
      An epitaph from Doctor Bowring !'

INTENTIONS

A REMONSTRANCE IN THE VENTILATOR

   Now don't abuse us, Fanny, don't,
      You're really too provoking ;
I won't sit by, I vow I won't,
      To hear your idle croaking :
You seem to think the world is mad
      For places and for pensions,
And won't believe—it's quite too bad—
      That Whigs have good intentions.

I know that Denman is too rash
And Graham not too witty;
I know we hear prodigious trash
From members for the City:
Young Thomson is a financier
Of rather small dimensions;
Lord Althorp is not vastly clear,
But all have bright intentions.

The Budget *was* a slight mistake,
You call it quite correctly;
But then confess, for candour's sake,
We gave it up directly.
They laughed it down on every side,
Forgetting their dissensions,
But not a single man denied
It showed the best intentions.

The Premier has been kind, I own,
To most of his connections;
But Hunt, you see, was quite alone
In making harsh reflections:
The blockhead ought to go to school,
And study his declensions;
Then he would judge by better rule
A statesman's grand intentions.

And, Fanny, as for this Reform,
　　Which Peel pronounces ' treason,'
Indeed I think you make a storm
　　Without sufficient reason :
The Bill is full of faults, no doubt ;
　　But, as my husband mentions,
One would not have a clause struck out,
　　Which flows from just intentions.

Some say the Bill destroys the crown ;
　　Some swear it gulls the people ;
Some see the peerage tumbling down ;
　　Some fear for church and steeple :
There may be good substantial cause
　　For many apprehensions ;
But *coûte qui coûte*, in every clause,
　　There's proof of right intentions.

We can't expect that Brougham and Hume
　　Will lay their horrid plans down ;
But, dearest love, you won't assume
　　The fault is with Lord Lansdowne !
They can't do harm ;—or if they do,
　　In spite of wise preventions,
I hate their scheme,—but, *entre nous*,
　　I honour their intentions.

REASONS FOR NOT RATTING

'Sound opinions are like sound wine ; they are the better for
keeping.'—LORD DUDLEY'S *Speech.*

IT was my father's wine ;—alas,
   It was his chiefest bliss,
To fill an old friend's evening glass
   With nectar such as this :
I think I have as warm a heart,
   As kind a friend, as he ;
Another bumper ere we part ;—
   Old wine, old wine for me !

In this we toasted William Pitt,
   Whom twenty now outshine ;
O'er this we laughed at Canning's wit
   Ere Hume's was thought as fine ;
In this the King, the Church, the Laws,
   Have had their three times three,
Sound wine befits as sound a cause ;
   Old wine, old wine for me !

In this, when France, in those long wars,
   Was beaten, black and blue,
We used to drink our troops and tars,
   Our Wellesley and Pellew :

Now things are changed ;—though Britain's fame
    May out of fashion be,
At least my wine remains the same ;—
    Old wine, old wine for me !

My neighbours, Robinson and Lamb,
    Drink French, of last year's growth ;
I'm sure, however they may sham,
    It disagrees with both ;
I don't pretend to interfere;
    An Englishman is free ;
But none of that cheap poison here ;—
    Old wine, old wine for me !

Some dozens have lost, I must allow,
    Something of strength and hue ;
And there are vacant spaces now,
    To be filled up with new.
And there are cobwebs round the bins,
    Which some don't like to see ;
If these are all my cellar's sins,
    Old wine, old wine for me !

THE OLD TORY

'Quo semel est imbuta recens, servabit edorem
Testa diu.'—HORACE.

AY, chatter, chatter, brother Sam ;
   Call Thomson deep and Sheil divine ;
And tell us all that Master Cam
   Is quite a Tully in his line.
I'm near threescore ; you ought to know
   You can't transplant so old a tree ;
I was a Tory long ago ;
   You'll hardly make a Whig of me.

Lord Palmerston may turn about,
   And curse the creed he held so long ;
And moral Grant may now find out
   That Canning was extremely wrong ;
Lansdowne with Waithman may unite,
   And Ministers with mobs agree ;
Truth may be falsehood, black grow white,
   But, Sir, you make no Whig of me.

You know I never learned to trust
   The wisdom of the Scotch Review ;
I worshipped not Napoleon's bust ;
   I could not blush for Waterloo ;

I'm proud of England's glory still,
   Of laurels won on land and sea;
Call me a bigot if you will
   But pray don't make a Whig of me.

I cannot march with Attwood's ranks,
   I cannot write with Russell's pen;
I have no longing for the thanks
   Of very loyal tithing-men;
I cannot wear a civil face
   When Carpue just drops in to tea;
I cannot flatter Mr. Place;
   You'll never make a Whig of me.

I can't admire the Bristol rows,
   Nor call the Common Council wise;
I cannot bow as Burdett bows,
   Nor lie as great O'Connell lies:
And if I wanted place or pay,
   A Baron's robe, or Bishop's see,
I'm not first cousin to Lord Grey;—
   Why should you make a Whig of me?

Good brother 'twere an easier thing
   To make a wit of Joseph Hume,
To make a conjuror of Lord King,
   To make a lawyer of Lord Brougham.

No, Howick will be half his sire,
   And Althorp learn the Rule of Three,
And Morpeth set the Thames on fire,
   Before you make a Whig of me !

LONG AGO

TO THE RIGHT HON. SIR JOHN CAM HOBHOUSE

WE were patriots together !—Oh, placeman and peer
   Are the patrons who smile on your labours to-day ;
And Lords of the Treasury lustily cheer
   Whatever you do, and whatever you say.
Go, pocket, my Hobhouse, as much as you will,
   The times are quite altered, we very well know :
But will you not, will you not, talk to us still,
   As you talked to us once, long ago, long ago ?

We were patriots together !—I know you will think
   Of the cobbler's caresses, the coalheaver's cries,
Of the stones that we threw, and the toasts that we
     drink,
   Of our pamphlets and pledges, our libels and lies !
When the truth shall awake, and the country and
     town
   Be heartily weary of Althorp and Co.,
My Hobhouse, come back to the Anchor and Crown,
   Let us be what we were, long ago, long ago.

PLUS DE POLITIQUE

IMITATED FROM DE BERANGER

No politics !—I cannot bear
   To tell our ancient fame ;
No politics !—I do not dare
   To paint our present shame.
What we have been, what we must be,
   Let other minstrels say ;
It is too dark a theme for me ;—
   No politics to-day.

I loved to see the captive's chain
   By British hands burst through ;
I loved to sing the fields of Spain,
   The war of Waterloo.
But now the Russians' greedy swords
   Are edged with English pay ;
We help, we hire, the robber hordes ;—
   No politics to-day.

I used to look on many a home
   Of industry and art ;
I gazed on pleasure's glorious dome,
   On labour's busy mart.

Q

From Derby's rows, from Bristol's fires,
    I turn with tears away ;
I can't admire what Brougham admires ;—
    No politics to-day.

I've often heard the faithless French
    Denounced by William Pitt ;
I've watched the flash from this same bench
    Of Canning's polished wit.
And when your Woods and Waithmans bawl,
    Your Humes and Harveys bray,
Good Lord ! I'm weary of them all ;—
    No politics to-day.

Let's talk of Coplestone and prayers,
    Of Kitchener and pies ;
Of Lady Sophonisba's airs,
    Of Lady Susan's eyes :
Let's talk of Mr. Attwood's cause,
    Of Mr. Pococke's play ;
Of fiddles, bubbles, rattles, straws ;—
    No politics to-day !

Let Joseph call religion ' cant,'
    While Warburton cries ' Hear ' ;
Let Charles Grant and Robert Grant
    Sit, *mutely* pious, near :

Let Durham and let Richmond vow
   They *never* will take pay,
N'importe, although they take it *now*,
   No politics to-day.

Let candid Althorp 'Budget' on,
   Sir Jemmy run his rig,
Let elderly Beau Palmerston
   Swear he was aye a Whig.
If poor Lord Liverpool could know,
   I wonder what he'd say ;
He served *him* twenty years or so ;—
   No politics to-day.

Let Birmingham give forth the law,
   St. Stephen's Hall be mute :
Let listening Unions pause in awe,
   While Bowring strikes the lute :
Let every rogue in every town
   Cry, 'Long live Brougham and Grey ;'
Let all the world turn upside down ;—
   No politics to-day.

A NURSERY SONG

'I had forgot Waterloo' (*Laughter*).
JOSEPH HUME.

HUME has been dotting and carrying one ;
Hume has been helping O'Connell and Son ;
Hume has been proving that wrong is right ;
Hume has been voting that black is white ;
Hume has so many things to do,
Hume has forgotten Waterloo.

Hume has been studying tare and tret ;
Hume has been summing the national debt ;
Hume has been babbling of silk and grain ;
Hume has been poring o'er Cocker and Paine ;
Hume is a sage and a patriot too ;
Hume has forgotten Waterloo.

Hume has been jobbing with infinite skill ;
Hume has been treating the poor Greeks ill ;
Hume has been rivalling Bowring's crimes ;
Hume has been chid in the fierce old *Times* ;
Hume has been reading the Yellow and Blue ;
Hume has forgotten Waterloo.

Hume for his toils has a wide, wide scope;
Hume is a friend to the friends of the Pope;
Hume has pleasure in Antwerp's fall;
Hume has an eye on Greece and Gaul;
Hume has a heart for a Quaker or Jew;
Hume has forgotten Waterloo.

Hume has been praising Bentham's schemes;
Hume has been puffing Thomson's dreams;
Hume has been hinting that piety's cant;
Hume has been frightening good Charles Grant;
Hume is to me what he is to you;
Hume has forgotten Waterloo.

STANZAS TO THE SPEAKER ASLEEP

SLEEP, Mr. Speaker; it's surely fair,
If you don't in your bed, that you should in your
    chair;
Longer and longer still they grow,
Tory and Radical, Aye and No;
Talking by night, and talking by day;—
Sleep, Mr. Speaker; sleep, sleep, while you may!

Sleep, Mr. Speaker; slumber lies
Light and brief on a Speaker's eyes;

Feilden or Finn, in a minute or two,
Some disorderly thing will do ;
Riot will chase repose away ;—
Sleep, Mr. Speaker ; sleep, sleep, while you may !

Sleep, Mr. Speaker ; Cobbett will soon
Move to abolish the Sun and Moon ;
Hume, no doubt, will be taking the sense
Of the House on a saving of thirteen pence ;
Grattan will growl, or Baldwin bray ;—
Sleep, Mr. Speaker ; sleep, sleep, while you may !

Sleep, Mr. Speaker ; dream of the time
When loyalty was not quite a crime ;
When Grant was a pupil in Canning's school ;
When Palmerston fancied Wood a fool ;
Lord, how principles pass away ;—
Sleep, Mr. Speaker ; sleep, sleep, while you may !

Sleep, Mr. Speaker ; sweet to men
Is the sleep that comes but now and then ;
Sweet to the sorrowful, sweet to the ill,
Sweet to the children that work in a mill ;
You have more need of sleep than they ;—
Sleep, Mr. Speaker ; sleep, sleep, while you may !

MAXIMS

'Lord Auckland is understood to be appointed permanently on Constitutional grounds.'—*Globe*, Jan. 14, 1834.

If a Tory is ever found out
    In pocketing twenty pence,
The thing is a job, no doubt,
    It admits of no defence:
If a Whig has the luck to secure
    Some twenty thousand pounds,
It is all arranged, be sure,
    On 'Constitutional grounds.'

If a Tory dares distrust
    The faith of our fiercest foe,
Suspicion is quite unjust,
    And jealousy vastly low:
If a Whig with a bold blockade
    Our ancient friend confounds,
It is done, for the good of trade,
    On 'Constitutional grounds.'

If a Tory punishes crimes
    In Kerry or in Clare,
The wisdom of the *Times*
    Proclaims it quite unfair:

If a Whig with a troop of horse
   The Murphys and Macs astounds,
He cuts and thrusts of course
   On 'Constitutional grounds.'

If a Tory gives a place
   To a nephew or a son,
Good lack! a thing so base
   Was never, never done !
If a Whig, with his countless kin,
   The nation's purse surrounds,
They slip their fingers in
   On 'Constitutional grounds.'

Then take, my Lord, oh, take
   The gift the Greys provide,
For the Constitution's sake,
   And for no ends beside.
And think, on quarter-day,
   Of the friend who thus expounds
The rights of place and pay
   On 'Constitutional grounds.'

THE STATE OF THE COUNTRY

'We are now a trampled nation.'
Times, March 10, 1834.

WE have been some years reforming,
Chattering, cheering, stamping, storming;
Cutting bludgeons from the hedges;
Asking for all sorts of pledges;
Breaking heads, and breaking glasses;
Calling people knaves and asses:
After all our agitation,
We are now a 'trampled nation'!

Mr. Croker's thrusts are parried;
Schedules A and B are carried;
Vain is Wetherell's long alarum;
There is no reprieve for Sarum:
All the money in our pockets—
Went to purchase squibs and rockets:
Oh, what foolish exultation!
We are still a 'trampled nation'!

Buckingham is quite a Tully;
Solon was a fool to Gully;
Pryme's a lecturer, taught at College;
Pease, a Quaker, full of knowledge;

Feilden is extremely clever ;
Finn can talk and talk for ever :
What a glorious constellation !
Yet we are a 'trampled nation.'

We have got Lord Grey to ease us
Of the taxes that displease us ;
We have got, besides, some dozens
Of his Lordship's sons and cousins ;
They are blest with places, pensions,
And the very best intentions ;
It's against their inclination
That we are a 'trampled nation.'

We have got the *Times* adorning
Facts with figures every morning ;
Now denouncing right and reason ;
Now defending guilt and treason ;
Raving, ranting, blustering, blundering,
Pro and *con* alternate thundering.
It has wondrous circulation !—
Why are we a 'trampled nation'?

EBENEZER ELLIOTT—CHARLES MACKAY

(I have thought it well to give a couple of samples of the Radical bards of the middle of the present century, though their verse be no great thing as a rule.)

BATTLE SONG

Day, like our souls, is fiercely dark ;
    What then ?   'Tis day !
We sleep no more ; the cock crows—hark !
    To arms ! away !
They come ! they come ! the knell is rung
    Of us or them ;
Wide o'er their march the pomp is flung
    Of gold and gem.
What collar'd hound of lawless sway,
    To famine dear—
What pension'd slave of Attila,
    Leads in the rear ?

Come they from Scythian wilds afar,
    Our blood to spill?
Wear they the livery of the Czar?
    They do his will.
Nor tassell'd silk, nor epaulette,
    Nor plume, nor torse—
No splendour gilds, all sternly met,
    Our foot and horse.
But, dark and still, we inly glow,
    Condens'd in ire!
Strike tawdry slaves, and ye shall know
    Our gloom is fire.
In vain your pomp, ye evil powers,
    Insults the land;
Wrongs, vengeance, and *the cause* are ours,
    And God's right hand!
Madmen! they trample into snakes
    The wormy clod!
Like fire beneath their feet awakes
    The sword of God!
Behind, before, above, below,
    They rouse the brave;
Where'er they go, they make a foe,
    Or find a grave.

THE GOOD TIME COMING

THERE'S a good time coming, boys,
 A good time coming :
We may not live to see the day,
But earth shall glisten in the ray
 Of the good time coming.
Cannon-balls may aid the truth,
 But thought's a weapon stronger ;
We'll win our battle by its aid ;—
 Wait a little longer.

There's a good time coming, boys,
 A good time coming :
The pen shall supersede the sword,
And Right, not Might, shall be the lord
 In the good time coming.
Worth, not Birth, shall rule mankind,
 And be acknowledged stronger ;
The proper impulse has been given ;—
 Wait a little longer.

There's a good time coming, boys,
 A good time coming :
War in all men's eyes shall be
A monster of iniquity
 In the good time coming :

Nations shall not quarrel then,
 To prove which is the stronger ;
Nor slaughter men for glory's sake ;—
 Wait a little longer.

There's a good time coming, boys,
 A good time coming :
Hateful rivalries of creed
Shall not make their martyrs bleed
 In the good time coming.
Religion shall be shorn of pride,
 And flourish all the stronger ;
And Charity shall trim her lamp ;—
 Wait a little longer.

There's a good time coming, boys,
 A good time coming :
And a poor man's family
Shall not be his misery
 In the good time coming.
Every child shall be a help,
 To make his right arm stronger ;
The happier he the more he has ;—
 Wait a little longer.

There's a good time coming, boys,
 A good time coming :

The Good Time Coming

Little children shall not toil,
Under, or above the soil,
    In the good time coming;
But shall play in healthful fields
    Till limbs and mind grow stronger;
And every one shall read and write;—
    Wait a little long longer.

There's a good time coming, boys,
    A good time coming:
The people shall be temperate,
And shall love instead of hate,
    In the good time coming.
They shall use and not abuse,
    And make all virtue stronger.
The reformation has begun;—
    Wait a little longer.

There's a good time coming, boys,
    A good time coming:
Let us aid it all we can,
Every woman, every man,
    The good time coming.
Smallest helps, if rightly given,
    Make the impulse stronger;
'Twill be •strong enough one day;—
    Wait a little longer.

WILLIAM MAKEPEACE THACKERAY

(To what has been said in the Introduction as to Thackeray's gifts for political verse I need add nothing, except that in the strict kind he was never so happy as on Irish matters. King Canute, great as it is, belongs perhaps rather to ethics than to politics.)

KING CANUTE

KING CANUTE was weary-hearted; he had reigned for
    years a score,
Battling, struggling, pushing, fighting, killing much
    and robbing more;
And he thought upon his actions, walking by the
    wild sea-shore.

'Twixt the Chancellor and Bishop walked the King
    with steps sedate,
Chamberlains and grooms came after, silversticks and
    goldsticks great,

Chaplains, aides-de-camp, and pages,—all the officers
of state.

Sliding after like his shadow, pausing when he chose
to pause,
If a frown his face contracted, straight the courtiers
dropped their jaws;
If to laugh the King was minded, out they burst in
loud hee-haws.

But that day a something vexed him, that was clear
to old and young:
Thrice his Grace had yawned at table, when his
favourite gleemen sung,
Once the Queen would have consoled him, but he
bade her hold her tongue.

'Something ails my gracious master,' cried the Keeper
of the Seal.
'Sure, my lord, it is the lampreys served to dinner, or
the veal?'
'Psha!' exclaimed the angry monarch. 'Keeper, 'tis
not that I feel.

''Tis the *heart*, and not the dinner, fool, that doth my
rest impair:
Can a king be great as I am, prithee, and yet know
no care?

R

Oh, I'm sick, and tired, and weary.'—Some one cried
    'The King's arm-chair!'.

Then towards the lackeys turning, quick my Lord the
    Keeper nodded,
Straight the King's great chair was brought him, by
    two footmen able-bodied;
Languidly he sank into it: it was comfortably wadded.

'Leading on my fierce companions,' cried he, 'over
    storm and brine,
I have fought and I have conquered! Where was
    glory like to mine?'
Loudly all the courtiers echoed: 'Where is glory like
    to thine?'

'What avail me of my kingdoms? Weary am I now
    and old;
Those fair sons I have begotten, long to see me dead
    and cold;
Would I were, and quiet buried, underneath the
    silent mould!

'Oh, remorse, the writhing serpent! at my bosom
    tears and bites;
Horrid, horrid things I look on, though I put out all
    the lights;
Ghosts of ghastly recollections troop about my bed at
    nights.

'Cities burning, convents blazing, red with sacrilegious
   fires ;
Mothers weeping, virgins screaming : vainly for the
   slaughtered sires.'—
'Such a tender conscience,' cries the Bishop, 'every
   one admires.

'But for such unpleasant bygones, cease, my gracious
   lord, to search,
They're forgotten and forgiven by our Holy Mother
   Church ;
Never, never does she leave her benefactors in the
   lurch.

'Look ! the land is crowned with ministers, which
   your Grace's bounty raised ;
Abbeys filled with holy men, where you and Heaven
   are daily praised :
You, my lord, to think of dying ? on my conscience
   I'm amazed ! '

'Nay, I feel,' replied King Canute, 'that my end is
   drawing near.'
'Don't say so,' exclaimed the courtiers (striving each
   to squeeze a tear).
'Sure your Grace is strong and lusty, and may live
   this fifty year.'

'Live these fifty years!' the Bishop roared, with actions
    made to suit.
'Are you mad, my good Lord Keeper, thus to speak
    of King Canute!
Men have lived a thousand years, and sure his
    Majesty will do't.

'Adam, Enoch, Lamech, Cainan, Mahaleel, Methusela,
Lived nine hundred years apiece, and mayn't the King
    as well as they?'
'Fervently,' exclaimed the Keeper, 'fervently I trust
    he may.'

'*He* to die?' resumed the Bishop. 'He a mortal
    like to *us*?
Death was not for him intended, though *communis
omnibus* :
Keeper, you are irreligious, for to talk and cavil thus.

'With his wondrous skill in healing ne'er a doctor
    can compete,
Loathsome lepers, if he touch them, start up clean
    upon their feet;
Surely he could raise the dead up, did his Highness
    think it meet.

'Did not once the Jewish captain stay the sun upon
    the hill,

And the while he slew the foemen, bid the silver
    moon stand still!
So, no doubt, could gracious Canute, if it were his
    sacred will.'

'Might I stay the sun above us, good Sir Bishop?'
    Canute cried;
'Could I bid the silver moon to pause upon her
    heavenly ride?
If the moon obeys my orders, sure I can command
    the tide.

'Will the advancing waves obey me, Bishop, if I
    make the sign?'
Said the Bishop, bowing lowly, 'Land and sea, my
    lord, are thine.'
Canute turned towards the ocean—'Back!' he said,
    'thou foaming brine.

'From the sacred shore I stand on, I command thee
    to retreat;
Venture not, thou stormy rebel, to approach thy
    master's seat:
Ocean, be thou still! I bid thee come not nearer to
    my feet!'

But the sullen ocean answered with a louder, deeper
    roar,

And the rapid waves drew nearer, falling sounding on
the shore ;
Back the Keeper and the Bishop, back the King and
courtiers bore.

And he sternly bade them never more to kneel to
human clay,
But alone to praise and worship that which earth and
seas obey :
And his golden crown of empire never wore he from
that day.
King Canute is dead and gone : Parasites exist alway.

THE BATTLE OF LIMERICK

Ye Genii of the nation,
Who look with veneration,
And Ireland's desolation onsaysingly deplore ;
Ye sons of General Jackson,
Who thrample on the Saxon,
Attend to the thransaction upon Shannon shore.

When William, Duke of Schumbug,
A tyrant and a humbug,
With cannon and with thunder on our city bore,
Our fortitude and valliance
Insthructed his battalions
To rispict the galliant Irish upon Shannon shore.

Since that capitulation,
No city in this nation
So grand a reputation could boast before,
As Limerick prodigious,
That stands with quays and bridges,
And the ships up to the windies of the Shannon shore.

A chief of ancient line,
'Tis William Smith O'Brine,
Reprisints this darling Limerick, this ten years or more:
O the Saxons can't endure
To see him on the flure,
And thrimble at the Cicero from Shannon shore!

This valliant son of Mars
Had been to visit Par's,
That land of Revolution, that grows the tricolor;
And to welcome his returrn
From pilgrimages furren,
We invited him to tay on the Shannon shore.

Then we summoned to our board
Young Meagher of the sword:
'Tis he will sheathe that battle-axe in Saxon gore;
And Mitchil of Belfast,
We bade to our repast,
To dthrink a dish of coffee on the Shannon shore.

Convaniently to hould
These patriots so bould,
We tuck the opportunity of Tim Doolan's store;
And with ornamints and banners
(As becomes gintale good manners)
We made the loveliest tay-room upon Shannon shore.

'Twould binifit your sowls,
To see the butthered rowls,
The sugar-tongs and sangwidges and craim galyore,
And the muffins and the crumpets,
And the band of harps and thrumpets,
To celebrate the sworry upon Shannon shore.

Sure the Imperor of Bohay
Would be proud to dthrink the tay
That Misthress Biddy Rooney for O'Brine did pour;
And, since the days of Strongbow,
There never was such Congo—
Mitchil dthrank six quarts of it—by Shannon shore.

But Clarndon and Corry
Connellan beheld this sworry
With rage and imulation in their black hearts' core;
And they hired a gang of ruffins
To interrupt the muffins,
And the fragrance of the Congo on the Shannon shore.

When full of tay and cake,
O'Brine began to spake,
But juice a one could hear him, for a sudden roar
Of a ragamuffin rout
Began to yell and shout,
And frighten the propriety of Shannon shore.

As Smith O'Brine harangued,
They batthered and they banged :
Tim Doolan's doors and windies, down they tore ;
They smashed the lovely windies
(Hung with muslin from the Indies),
Purshuing of their shindies upon Shannon shore.

With throwing of brickbats,
Drowned puppies, and dead rats,
These ruffin democrats themselves did lower ;
Tin kettles, rotten eggs,
Cabbage-stalks, and wooden legs,
They flung among the patriots of Shannon shore.

O the girls began to scrame,
And upset the milk and crame ;
And the honourable gintlemin, they cursed and swore :
And Mitchil of Belfast,
'Twas he that looked aghast,
When they roasted him in effigy by Shannon shore.

O the lovely tay was spilt
On that day of Ireland's guilt;
Says Jack Mitchil, 'I am kilt!   Boys, where's the
      back door?
'Tis a national disgrace;
Let me go and veil me face;'
And he boulted with quick pace from the Shannon
      shore.

'Cut down the bloody horde!'
Says Meagher of the sword,
'This conduct would disgrace any blackamore:'
But the best use Tommy made
Of his famous battle blade
Was to cut his own stick from the Shannon shore.

Immortal Smith O'Brine
Was raging like a line;
'Twould have done your sowl good to have heard him
      roar;
In his glory he arose,
And he rush'd upon his foes,
But they hit him on the nose by the Shannon shore.

Then the Futt and the Dthragoons
In squadthrons and platoons,
With their music playing chunes, down upon us bore;
And they bate the rattatoo,
But the Peelers came in view,
And ended the shaloo on the Shannon shore.

HENRY LONGUEVILLE MANSEL

(The late Dean Mansel's Phrontisterion, *the most excellent piece of university wit produced in this century at least, was composed on the first Oxford Commission, and is in great part a severe satire on its interference with university and collegiate endowments. But the author was a very strong Tory, and it frequently diverges, as here, into matter of wider application.)*

PHRONTISTERION

SCENE III

(Enter Just Discourse and Unjust Discourse)

U. D.—Where be they, the dreaming dotards, bigots of the olden time,
Purblind patrons of abuses, champions of corruption's slime,
Pudding-headed, narrow-minded, noddynoodledoodle-nincom—

Poops, who doubt our right of dealing as we please
    with college income?

    J. D.—Where be they, the shameless spoilers, vio-
    lating private right,

Riding roughshod over justice, crushing equity with
    might,

Turning from its proper channels wealth our fathers'
    bounty left,

Sullying reform with rapine, public ends with private
    theft?

    U. D.—Theft, my friend! the gods have pity on
    your weak and watery brain!

How can they who own the total steal a portion?
    pray explain.

Men in nature's state are equal: property, conferred
    by laws,

From the sanction of the people all its rights and
    safeguards draws.

You but hold it at their pleasure, you must yield it at
    their summons:

And the pleasure of the people, seek it in the House
    of Commons.

    J. D.—Have you then no higher standards, fixed
    ere human laws began

By the voice of man's Creator, by the moral sense of
    man?

Rules may alter, codes may perish, customs change,
    but these abide,

Truths no practice can abolish, no enactment over-
 ride.
Vain the fine-drawn web of sophisms, vain the brazen
 mail of lies ;
Means condemned by God and Conscience, no ex-
 pedience justifies.
 U. D.—Moral sense ! a mere delusion : prejudice
 of education ;
Amiable in individuals, childish weakness in a nation.
Pious scruples, tender conscience, doubtless suit a
 private station ;
Public interest's the rule for all enlightened legislation.
So in debts : one's private duty pleads, perhaps, for
 liquidation :
In a free enlightened people, who shall blame repudia-
 tion ?
 J. D.—Yet bethink thee that the spirit whence those
 pious bounties flowed
To the ties of private feeling all its force and being
 owed.
Severed from the bonds of kindred, taught his lonely
 heart to school
By his Father's chastening kindness or his Church's
 sterner rule,
Oft to spots by memory cherished, where his earliest
 love began,
In his age's desolation, fondly turned the childless
 man.

Then the quickening drops of kindness through the
　　drooping soul were felt
From the home his youth that nurtured, from the
　　church where first he knelt.
Then the long-neglected feelings claimed once more
　　their moving part,
And the pent-up tide of bounty forced its passage
　　through the heart.
　　U. D.—Stuff and nonsense! why should feeling
　　public spirit clog and cumber.
When the greatest happiness is wanted for the greatest
　　number?
Private ties, you can't disprove it if you argue to
　　eternity,
Hamper in their narrow fetters Cosmopolitan Frater-
　　nity.
Close Foundations, limited to one particular locality,
Might as well be left to foster open vice and immor-
　　ality :
I should feel far more compunction, laying hands to
　　spoil and pillage
On the brothel of an empire than the college of a
　　village.
　　J. D.—Shameless Robber !
　　U. D.　　　　　　　　　Owl-eyed Bigot !
　　J. D.　　　　　　　　　　　　　Hear'st thou
　　Heaven, and sleeps thy thunder?
Right Divine proclaimed for rapine, Laws invoked to
　　sanction plunder !

Take a warning in thy triumph.   Godless power is
    frail to trust :
Sure the millstone of his vengeance ; late it grinds,
    but grinds to dust.
Search the tale of fallen nations.   Justice banished,
    rights forgot.
History's record tells the sequel.   Seek her place, and
    she is not.
    U. D.—Worn out notions, musty fancies, redolent
    of Church and king,
Guardian-Angels, George-and-Dragons, that old-
    fashioned sort of thing.
Master spirits, leading statesmen, all to circumstances
    bow :
Public Conscience, State Religion, even Gladstone
    scouts them now.
Tut, man, look to facts and figures : truce to all this
    idle bustle :
Bluff King Hal is praised in Christchurch ; plundered
    Woburn breeds a Russell.
Look at France's half-fledged eaglet, gazing with un-
    dazzled eye
On the sunbeams of his glory,—and the Orleans
    property.
Look at Prussia's champion-heroes, men in freedom's
    tale immortal,
Chalking 'national possession' on their tyrant's
    palace portal.

Look at England's Church Commission, holy work
    by Bishops blest

Half your Chapters burked already; Blandford's bill
    will do the rest.

If you bandy rights and duties, great reforms will
    ne'er begin.

Give the cards a thorough shuffle : cut again; first
    knave to win.

    J. D.—'Tis in vain, I see, to argue. Modern light
    must have its way.

Public morals sapped and rotted, knaves must even
    win the day.

Fare thee well. Should after-ages bring to pass the
    scene foretold,

When our future is a memory, and our days are days
    of old.

When New Zealand's travelled native from some
    ruined arch looks down

On old Thames's silent current, London's desolated
    town.

On the banks no groaning warehouse, on the stream
    no flag unfurled,

Where the modern Carthage traded long ago with half
    a world.

Then if History's bitter lesson wake the patriot's
    anxious care,

Thus the warning voice may mingle in the accents of
    his prayer.

Thou that holds the fate of nations in the scales of
 Justice weighed,

Not alone 'gainst foreign armies ; 'gainst ourselves we
 ask thy aid.

Never may my country's counsels traffic's sordid spirit
 feel,

Selling birthrights, cheapening pottage, trading with
 a nation's weal.

Never may a craven pilot at our vessel's helm preside,

Swayed by mob-tongued agitation, taking demagogues
 for guide,

Truckling to the voice of faction, listening for the
 loudest cry,

Gauging pressures, measuring noises, what to grant
 and what deny.

Never may the scoundrel maxims of a money-making
 band

Pawn the charter of our freedom, blight the sinews of
 our land.

Thou whose gifts are might and wisdom, purge from
 mists my country's eyes ;

Teach her in the hour of trial where alone her safety
 lies ;

Bid her scorn the shout of faction, bid her spurn the
 lust of pelf,

Trusting still through good and evil in her God and
 in herself.

S

And if ever public feeling, led by selfish tongues
    astray,
Gloat o'er traffic's heaped-up riches, smile when Church
    and State decay,
Though our blindness ask out curses, still do Thou
    vouchsafe to bless,
Spare us England's tradesmen-senate, spare her cotton-
    spun success.

HENRY DUFF TRAILL

(Of whom, as happily living, I shall say no more than that I owe him my best thanks for permitting me to fish in his abundant and lucent streams, which still flow, but from the freshest of which I have, for reasons, not drawn. The three pieces here given are taken from Recaptured Rhymes.*)*

LAPUTA OUTDONE

OH, Philosopher crazed from the Island of Crazes,
  Explored and depicted by Jonathan Swift,
Let us hear what your judgments on us and our ways
    is—
Permit us your mental impressions to sift.

For *we* have our follies of wisdom fantastic,
  Some high-philosophic, political some,
And would fain ascertain, in no spirit sarcastic,
  If you, my dear pundit, can match them at home.

When a man in Laputa falls sick unto danger,
    Then is it the rule in that singular place
To throw up the window and ask the first stranger
    To kindly come in and prescribe on the case?

When in legal perplexities, slighter or deeper,
    For counsel in law a Laputan applies,
Does he seek the next crossing and beg of its sweeper,
    When business is done, to step round and advise?

Are your pilots' certificates commonly given
    To men who have not even looked on the seas?
Are your coachmen selected for not having driven?
    Say, have you Laputans got customs like these?

You haven't?   Then off with your bee-bearing bonnet,
    Illustrious guest from Luggnaggian shores!
And down on your knee and do homage upon it
    Profound to a State that is madder than yours!

For though we select not attorney, physician,
    Or pilot who steers us, or coachman who drives,
From the ignorant crowd, who would gain erudition
    At risk of our fortunes, our limb, or our lives;

Yet this Ignorance dense that we do not let lead us
    In private concerns, lest disaster befall,

This, that may not make wills for us, dose us, or bleed
    us
May *rule* us—the business that's hardest of all !

We say to It 'Courage !   Nay, go not so shyly !
    In time you will master the work you are at ;
Your country presents you her own *corpus vile*,
    See, here is the commonwealth, practise on that !

' Away with the notion (we echo in chorus)
    Of power withheld until knowledge be gained,'
(Too long, cry the carts, have the horses before us
    Unjust and unworthy precedence obtained !)

' The use of the scalpel in surgical functions
    Will give you the skill of a surgeon professed,
And by much engine-driving at intricate junctions
    One learns to drive engines along with the best.'

For is it not thus our political preachers
    Discourse to us daily, in bidding us note
That ' the franchise itself is the truest of teachers,'
    That ' voting instructs in the use of the vote '?

So, off with it !   Off with your bee-bearing bonnet,
    Illustrious guest from Luggnaggian shores !
And down on your knee, and do homage upon it
    Profound to a State that is madder than yours !

BALLAD OF BALOONATICS CRANIOCRACS

OF all the accomplished Professors who ever
From learning contrived common-sense to dissever—
Of all who delight, on a question of tongue,
To foment agitation the peoples among—
None goes with such thoroughness into the thing
As the erudite Slav whose proceedings I sing ;
And whose name—if your jaws I may venture to tax—
Is Professor Baloonatics Craniocracs.

International law has his sovereign contempt ;
From restraints of political prudence exempt,
He holds that when races for union clamour,
The question's but one of comparative grammar.
No 'national movement,' whatever its fruits,
That starts from a real relation of roots,
The strenuous aid and encouragement lacks
Of the famous philologist, Craniocracs.

To many a cause of the 'national' sort
The Professor has lent his enlightened support ;
But of all his distinctions, his pride was to be a
High priest of the Pan-Macaronic Idea,

And first to have raised the Spaghettian claim
To inherit the true Macaronian name :
A position sustained against many attacks
By Professor Baloonatics Craniocracs.

The Spaghetts had been living in decent content, a
Race subject for centuries past to Polenta,
With liberties local and customs respected,
And lenient taxes with justice collected,
And ample permission their children to teach
That poetic and grandly cacophonous speech
Which first to their true nationality's tracks
Had directed Baloonatics Craniocracs.

But they, when he set their ethnology right,
With the free Macaronians burned to unite :
And the worthy Professor went round through their
     cities
Establishing Pan-Macaronic Committees,
Until they rebelled in a war to the knife,
And after two years of the bloodiest strife,
Forced haughty Polenta her grasp to relax,
To the joy of their champion Craniocracs.

From this struggle the rise of the Union dates
Of the Pan-Macaronic Confederate States,
Which, besides the Spaghetts, of a kindred as true
Raviolians counts and Lasagnians too.

But above them the Pateditalians claim
A supremacy, due to generical name ;
And their claim the Professor unswervingly backs,
For philologist always is Craniocracs.

Are the freed populations content with their lot ?
Well, candour compels me to say they are not.
Already the Union is deeply in debt
And taxed to the skin is the wretched Spaghett.
And the Pateditalians forbid him to teach
His poetic and grandly cacophonous speech,
On the ground that of modern corruption it smacks—
As is even admitted by Craniocracs.

But the worst of it is (if the murder must out),
The Professor's researches have led him to doubt
If his first ethnologic conclusions were sound,
Since he, as it seems, a new 'factor' has found,
The 'Vermicellenic,' so named from a race
Whose affinities throw a new light on the case ;
Transforming, indeed, into whites all its blacks
To the mind of Baloonatics Craniocracs.

Through the Vermicellenes the Spaghett and his
    brother,
Are clearly of kin to Polenta and other
Great nations ; and though they could only unite
By involving the world in a general fight,

The Professor, intrepid of logic as ever,
Will work day and night at that noble endeavour.
All hobbies are wild, but the wildest of hacks
Is bestrid by Baloonatics Craniocracs.

TO A FAMOUS PARLIAMENT

Hunc neque dira venena nec hosticus auferet ensis
Nec laterum dolor aut tussis nec tarda podagra ;
Garrulus hunc quando consumet cumque ; loquace
Si sapiat, vitet, simul atque adoleverit ætas.

As one who from the glacier past the vine
Follows the slow debasement of the Rhine
To where its foiled and sluggish waters creep
Through sand-obstructed channels to the deep—
As such an one may in fantastic mood
Muse on the checkered fortunes of the flood,
The source majestic whence its streams descend,
Its proud career and its ignoble end,—
Thus—but in sober earnestness—are we,
O English Parliament, to think of thee ?
Of thee on flats of dull Obstruction found
The long-descended and the high-renowned !
O thou whose shame or glory is our own,
Born with our birth, and with our growth upgrown !
Was it for this the wasting hand of time,
Perils of youth, and maladies of prime,

Spared thee so long?   O thou who first didst draw
In a rude age the infant breath of law,
And, storing silent increments of life
Through our long era of dynastic strife,
Take gradual heart of grace thy voice to raise
From whispering humbleness of Tudor days;
Wrest the high sceptre from thy Stuart lords;
Bend only for an hour to Cromwell's swords;
Live faction down, break through corruption's chains,
And of the Walpole-poison purge thy veins;
Wax stronger and still stronger, till the land
Saw all its forces gathered to thine hand—
Didst thou thus triumph that thou thus shouldst fall?
Is that proud head that towers over all
Destined to bow before unworthy foes?
Had ever splendid life so mean a close
As thine will show, if thou, for all thy past,
Must die of talk and Irishmen at last?

NOTES

P. 1.

Fraine, or better, *frayne* = 'ask.'   A.-S. *fregnan*.

P. 2.

Tancrete, O. F. *tancrit*, a queer form, as Professor Skeat observes to me, for 'transcript.'

P. 3.

Undermynde, of course = undermine.
Coarted = coerced.

P. 4.

Acisia (or rather *accidia*) is a mediæval corruption of ἀκηδία, used for that deadly sin which we rather inadequately translate Sloth, and which signifies properly a brutal and hardened indifference to the dictates of reason and conscience.
Sygne we, *i.e.* cross ourselves.
Amamelek = a mameluke (?) or diabolical (?)

P. 5.

Sanke roiall, 'blood royal'; a coarse gibe, but not a bad one.
Parde = pardieu, 'forsooth.'
Quatriuials . . . triuials.—These (the proper form of the former being 'quadrivials') were the well-known 'Seven Liberal Arts' of the Middle Ages—Grammar, Logic, and Rhetoric formed the *Trivium*; Music, Arithmetic, Geometry, and Astronomy the *Quadrivium*.

P. 14.

Emanuel.—This College in Cambridge was founded avowedly for the propagation of Puritanism by Sir H. Mildmay; and it long continued a fountain-head thereof.

P. 27.

When aged Thames.—A reference (it may be barely necessary to remind the reader) to the 'Marriage of Thames and Medway' in the Fourth Book of the *Faërie Queene*.
Steward.—Miss Stewart of the 'little Roman nose.'

P. 28.

Pett.—The ingenious but unlucky Commissioner of that name.

P. 30.

A medal with the legend *Latamur* was actually struck in Shaftesbury's honour when the grand jury ignored the Bill of High Treason against him in November 1681. *Polish* refers to a gibe (of not clearly known original authority) against him, to the effect that he had thought of putting in for the Crown of

Poland when John Sobieski was elected some years earlier. The whole poem is a ferocious, but not absolutely false, satire on his very remarkable history and character.

P. 35.

In order to bring the poem within compass, some hundred lines or so have been omitted.

Stum.—New and as yet incompletely fermented wine used to freshen up stale. In the days when wine was almost always drunk from the cask this was an easy trick, and the mixture was very unwholesome.

P. 41.

D——y, etc., Danby, Sunderland, Godolphin.
L——y, 'Lory,' is Lawrence Hyde, Lord Rochester.

P. 43.

It is hardly necessary to fill in 'James' and 'Sancroft.'

P. 44.

Two Wives.—The nonjuring and 'juring' churches.
Clancarty.—'Lady Clancarty' has been dramatised.
T——n, Tillotson.

P. 46.

T——ton, Torrington, to wit, Herbert. The reference is to the unlucky battle of Beachy Head, wherein, I believe, modern naval critics think the admiral not so much to blame as Whigs, and not Whigs only, used to hold.

P. 62.

Celia.—Madame de Maintenon.

P. 66.

Bastimentos, lit. 'buildings.'—The forts and Treasury establishments at Portobello.

P. 68.

This exquisite piece ('Here lies Fred') is given with slight variations in different places; but this is, on the whole, the best version. I do not think the author has ever been identified.

P. 93.

Whitehead.—'Paul the Aged,' a clever fellow, but a very great scoundrel, chiefly famous, or infamous, for sharing in the Medmenham orgies. I do not know that he was much less clever or a much greater scoundrel than Churchill; but he did not write such good verses. On no account to be confounded with *William* Whitehead, his contemporary and junior by only five years, a poet laureate, a most respectable person, and one o the worst poets possible.

P. 94.

It would be a bad compliment to the reader to tell him anything about Shelburne, Wilkes, Bute, or Holland, but the modest worth of John Calcraft may be forgotten. His origin is disputed; he rose to enormous wealth by placemanship, borough-mongering, army agency, contracting, and playing fast and loose with the Pitt and Fox factions in the middle of the last century, and he was a great patron of Francis and (*seu potius* 'or') Junius. The English peerage escaped him by his death at the age of forty-six.

P. 95.

Sir Fletcher Norton, the Attorney-General, afterwards Lord Grantley.

P. 100.

It is barely necessary to remind the reader that Margaret Nicholson was an old mad woman who made an attempt on the life of George the Third.

P. 101.

This friendly sketch of the members of Pitt's government would require a treatise to expound it all ; nor is exposition very necessary, for the points are obvious enough.

P. 104.

Bulse.—The technical term for a package of diamonds, which Hastings was fabled by the Whigs as distributing to the Court and the Tories. The *dear Major* is Scott, as to whom see below.

Eden, afterwards Lord Auckland, and even more savagely libelled in an extract to be met with further on. *Takes his plate* refers to a pleasant old custom by which an ambassador was supplied with a service of silver plate at the expense of the country.

What, what !—George the Third's well-known catchword.

P. 105.

Beaufoy.—A great distiller, ancestor, I believe, of a present M.P. who is on the other side.

The Doctor.—Addington.

This book.—Referring to the famous 'general warrant' business with the North Briton, etc.

P. 106.

Jamie.—I suppose Thomson.

Major John Scott.—This was the person whom Hastings was so left to himself as to make his parliamentary mouthpiece. He appears to have possessed a combination of all the qualities which even in these degenerate days make a man loathsome to the House of Commons.

P. 109.

The original note on *sniff*, 'a new interjection for the sense of smelling,' is curious. The *Squad* were Hastings's parliamentary party.

Burgage.—Referring of course to the burgage tenure of most rotten boroughs.

P. 110.

This rondeau ascribed to Dr. Lawrence, the chief author of the *Rolliad*, is interesting for more than its matter. Lawrence was one of the very few writers of the form between Cotton in the seventeenth century, and its resumers in the last quarter of the nineteenth.

P. 111.

His Grace of Portland, between whom and Pitt a coalition was being negotiated by Mr. Powis. It was to be 'on fair and equal terms'; and the sting lies in the reproach of indifference to female charms constantly brought against Pitt by the wits.

P. 117.

Mother Schwellenberg, that terrible 'mother of the maids,' whom all lovers of Miss Burney curse, and whom Wolcot pursued even more unrelentingly than he did her master and mistress. This piece was written when the general dread of French Jacobinism enabled the Government to draw the reins tighter. But Wolcot, so far as I know, was never in the least interfered with.

P. 119.

R—s.—I confess ignorance of the four R—s; three only were taught me.

The L——.—Wolcot's longest satire on the Court—a satire which would be more amusing if it were shorter and cleaner.

P. 120.

When Pitt.—In 1801.

G——.— Grosvenor (?)

P. 129.

Acme and Septimius.—The previous selections from the *Anti-Jacobin* are either Canning's or the joint work of Canning, Ellis, and Frere. This is believed to be Ellis's own.

P. 130.

Indian, alluding to Fox's defeat on the India Bill.

N—rf—lk.—The third Duke was a violent Whig (he pro posed 'the Majesty of the People' at a public dinner) and a renowned toper.

P. 131.

Catherine of Russia had put Fox's bust in this proud position. There is a quiver of genuine indignation and a stateliness of march about these lines which would make them interesting in any case. They are still more so if, as is stated on the authority of Boswell, they are the work of Pitt himself.

P. 132.

The Progress of Man directly satirises Payne Knight, but indirectly also Darwin, and a large and vague body of philosophic Jacobins.

P. 134.

On Sundays cried.—By legal exception, as being exceptionally perishable.

P. 137.

Housekeeper.—The heroine of the once seemingly immortal *Stranger*, which now, but for *Pendennis*, would be wellnigh forgotten.

P. 138.

Last line—*Pictis puppibus.*

P. 139.

The d——d invalid Lieutenant's name was Price. The attempt on the isle of Marcou or Marcouf was made on 6th May 1798.

P. 144.

The nameless Bard was Mathias of the *Pursuits of Literature*, a book much more highly thought of in its own day than since.

P. 152.

Olmutz . . . him.—La Fayette.

P. 155.

Lame artificer.—Talleyrand.

P. 157.

Top line.—These blanks are explained in the original to be left on purpose, that each age may fill them in as it likes.

P. 164.

Sir David—Baird.

P. 166.

The statesman—Addington.

P. 179.

Mina—The Spaniard.

P. 205.

The Chancellor—Eldon.

P. 216.

Joe, Hume ; *Jerry*, Bentham.

P. 217.

Bowring—Sir John, once almost famous, now half-forgotten.

218.

Thomson.—Poulett Thomson, with whose name books take liberties.   Even Praed seems to have written 'Thompson.'

P. 219.

Coûte qui coûte is kitchen French, but I fear Praed wrote it.

P. 222.

Waithman—Alderman, butt-general to the Tory wits.

THE END

Printed by R. & R. CLARK, *Edinburgh*

www.ingramcontent.com/pod-product-compliance
Lightning Source LLC
Chambersburg PA
CBHW031407270326
41929CB00010BA/1356